Rene
by in
in pe
by p

# HOW TO MAKE YOUR OWN
# Drinks
## SUSY ATKINS

# HOW TO MAKE YOUR OWN

## Drinks

### SUSY ATKINS

MITCHELL BEAZLEY

First published in 2011 by Mitchell Beazley,
an imprint of Octopus Publishing Group Ltd,
Endeavour House, 189 Shaftesbury Avenue,
London WC2H 8JY
www.octopusbooks.co.uk
An Hachette UK Company www.hachette.co.uk

Distributed in the United States and Canada by
Octopus Books USA, 237 Park Avenue, New York,
NY 10017 USA

ISBN: 978 1 84533 583 0
Printed and bound in China

MADE BY

Commissioning Editors
**Hilary Lumsden**
**Tracey Smith**

Art Direction,
Illustration and Design
**Pene Parker**

Photography
**Noel Murphy**

Senior Editor
**Sybella Stephens**

Text Editor
**Hilary Lumsden**

Production Manager
**Peter Hunt**

# CONTENTS

How to Make Your Own
Drinks

SUSY ATKINS

PHOTOGRAPHY BY
NOEL MURPHY

Coffea
Arabica

# INTRODUCTION

Do you grow your own fruit and vegetables, or pick wild berries
and flowers? Or do you simply have a well-stocked kitchen, fridge
and freezer? I'll bet you care about using natural, fresh ingredients
in your cooking. So why, then, do we put up with such awful
shop-bought drinks? The usual trip up the shop aisle is pretty
unappetizing these days (apart from the table wines), with rows
of cheap, bland spirits, sickly and commercial liqueurs, and fiercely
fizzy, lurid 'soft' options. There are exceptions, of course, but
high-quality labels are rare, and they can be horribly expensive.

So let's make our own drinks out of natural, fresh – and often free –
ingredients, just as we do when cooking food. I've made a point of
using home-grown, foraged, or locally sourced, cheap ingredients
thoughout this book to create a diverse selection of tempting drinks
recipes. And how delicious they've turned out to be: family-friendly
cordials from flowers and fruit; fashionable spirit infusions for
cocktails and shots; rich liqueurs; hot and cold drinks based on fresh
herbs and dried spices. All of these can be made in a ridiculously
short time and are quite delectable. Meanwhile, the transformation
wrought by fermenting fruit, veg, honey, and even weeds and leaves
is nature at its most magical.

This is a straightforward, no-nonsense introduction to drinks-making
at home. Most of your core ingredients are out in the fields,
hedgerows and gardens, there for the taking. Let's get started.

## The garden and the orchard

It takes a small but significant mind-shift to start making drinks (instead of food) from home-grown produce. You've perhaps never thought of making wine out of your much treasured rhubarb – only crumbles or fruit fools. Blackcurrants are for pies and jam, but what about cordials or crème de cassis? Start eyeing your crops in a different way – especially those that regularly produce a glut.

For drinks-making, the most suitable home-grown ingredients include: strawberries, raspberries, blackcurrants, gooseberries, rhubarb, damsons, apples, pears, plums, parsnips, red chillies and various herbs. I've created drinks, soft and alcoholic, from all these and more – after raiding our own vegetable patch and begging quinces, grapes (and honey) from generous neighbours. Indeed, there's a great tip for making drinks from lovely fresh, local produce: ask around and see what else is ripening in nearby gardens and allotments. You might not grow raspberries or damsons yourself, but there's a good chance that someone who lives close by does. Be prepared to swap your own produce or finished drinks to get the core ingredients you need, but whether it's homemade or bartered, these basic supplies should cost you very little.

Of course for city-dwellers, life just isn't like that, but ingredients featured in this book that are easy to grow in a small backyard or even on a spacious, sunny balcony include: strawberries, grapes, rhubarb, chillies and herbs. Again, find out which of your friends and neighbours have city allotments, maybe offering to help out there in exchange for precious crops.

# Buying from farmers' markets and local shops

Large supermarkets and high-street greengrocers stock all the key ingredients needed in this book, both fresh produce and 'dry' items, such as sugar as well as store-cupboard spices and dried herbs. Look out for organic fruit and veg (always preferable, especially when the produce is not going to be peeled in the recipe), try to pick fruit and veg from the country (even better, the region) where you live, and check very carefully for freshness before buying, smelling and prodding along the way, if you can get away with it! Choose unwaxed citrus fruit. Special offers are great news here, providing a cheap source when you bulk-buy one particular item for a wine or cordial.

Do support farmers' markets, a hugely useful source of high-quality, locally grown fruit and veg – sometimes organic, and always in season. Farmers have 'gluts' of seasonal produce, too, so look out for cheap and plentiful supplies of all the essential fresh ingredients at particular times of the year and make the most of the harvest. Visiting a farmers' market is an especially appealing way to shop, and it's great to support local small businesses.

## ENSURING YOU USE THE BEST-QUALITY PRODUCE

1 Always use unsprayed fruit and vegetables to avoid getting chemical residues in the finished drinks.

2 Try natural pest controls, such as crushed eggshells, salt or copper rings on your vegetable beds.

3 Use netting to protect any fruit bushes and trees that are regularly raided by birds or other animals.

4 Pick home-grown produce only when it is properly ripe.

5 Remove any rotten or badly bruised parts of the fruit and give it all a really thorough wash to get rid of any soil or natural nasties before using.

# Getting ideas and inspiration

So, you're busy gathering in lots of lovely natural ingredients, and have all the many recipes that follow here to kick-start a brand-new, delicious pursuit. It's worth suggesting now, at this early stage, that you keep your eyes peeled for various other sources of drinks-making inspiration in order to build up a solid framework of reference. So, when you're harvesting crops and getting your kit together, bear in mind the following:

Make friends with your local brew-shop owner. There's bound to be an outlet selling home-brew kits nearby and it pays to get to know the people selling it, as they often have years of experience and sensible advice to offer. I used to pitch up at my local store regularly with a bundle of questions. The long-suffering owner passed on a great deal of knowledge, sometimes while selling me little more than a plastic airlock (thanks, Ian, by the way!).

Pester family, friends and neighbours for their own ideas. Wines, ciders, meads and spirit infusions in particular are ancient traditions, and have evolved in different regions and countries with slight (or more radical) variations, mostly to use specific, locally grown fruits and vegetables. So often it's the people living around you who provide inspiration. A notice in the local shop window or an advert in your regional magazine are other ways to find fellow drinks-makers. And family members may have old recipes squirreled away and should be delighted to pass them on.

Search out old books in second-hand bookshops and libraries. Although little has been written on drinks-making lately, the 1960s–80s proved to be a 'golden age' for this subject. There are plenty of dog-eared, wine-stained books from this era still kicking about, which might prove interesting (although some of the old photography is spectacularly off-putting!).

Do use the internet for tips on drinks-making by all means, but exercise caution. There are some useful websites out there (some are listed on page 156), but there are other, rather pointless ones too, and a few that are just plain whacky. Be selective.

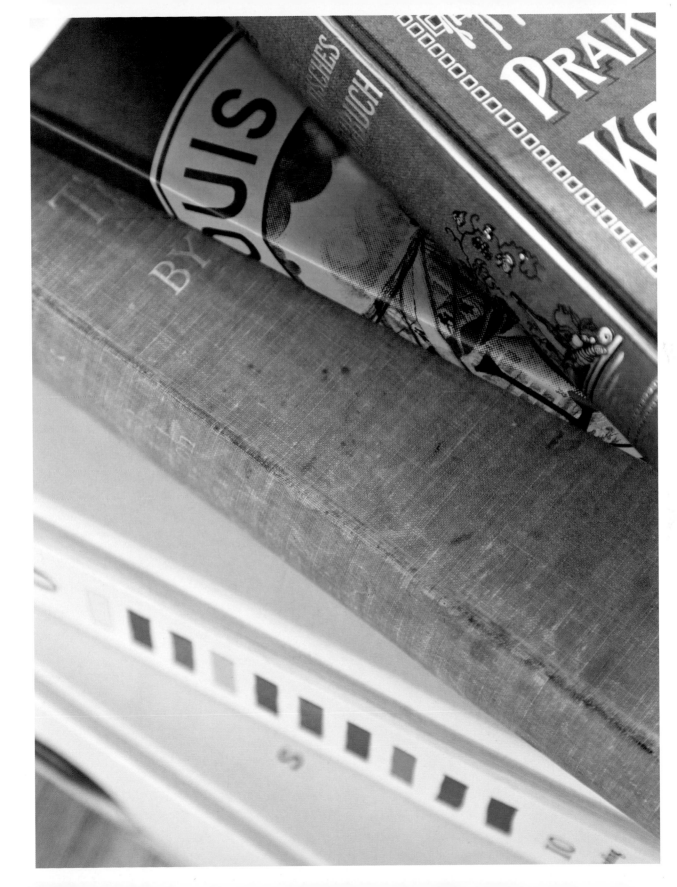

# Preserved fruit and vegetables

Out of season, the pickings can look a little thin. Do you really want to make wine out of slightly sad, underripe fruit that has been flown halfway across the world? You might as well buy cheap Chardonnay from the same place. At the farmers' market in winter the main crops may be leeks or red cabbage – even I'm not going to suggest you start fermenting those! So 'out of season' is when you might want to consider using frozen or tinned fruit and veg to make wine.

With a few provisos, go for it. Frozen fruit is particularly good. I have made plenty of drinks out of frozen currants, elderberries, blackberries, damsons and gooseberries in particular and the quality has been fine. Frozen strawberries and raspberries are somewhat less successful for making wine, but they will create reasonable soft drinks and infusions. Sloes are even better after a quick freeze (see page 76). Parsnips can certainly be used after freezing (freeze as raw chunks, see page 105). Tinned and bottled fruit can be considered – a decent cherry brandy or cherryade can be made from tinned cherries, for example (see page 140) – but in general fresh is definitely superior.

Wine made out of dried fruits, including apricots, sultanas, raisins and even figs, is possible, but do consult a specialist book for this. I prefer the flavours of fresh rather than dried fruit in my drinks, and this book contains only one wine with a dried fruit in it: Rice and Raisin Wine (see page 108). But there's nothing to stop you from experimenting.

# Foraging for ingredients

There's an argument for saying that foraging for your own is even better than growing your own! Let nature do the hard work, and when the hedgerow fruits or wild leaves are at their best, get out on a sunny day and grab them from the wild. I say 'sunny' quite deliberately. Wild crops tend to taste better if picked on a bright, dry day than when it's dark and damp; flowers in particular will have a much better aroma.

Get properly dressed to go foraging. We're talking long-sleeved T-shirts, long trousers, sturdy shoes or boots, gloves and even a hat. Sounds over the top? Not really. It's a strange thing, but most of the wild ingredients featured in these pages seem to grow in the midst of thorns, or surrounded by stinging nettles, or else they're high up a tall tree, or on a steep slope or buried in a hedgerow. Unless you're a giant, you'll be pulling down high branches to get to certain crops, bringing down leaves, twigs and insects on your head. So be prepared and cover up! Oh, and make sure to have bite- and sting-relief cream to hand (for inevitable insect and plant stings).

Take plenty of plastic bags and containers for bringing your crops home, and if driving a long way on a hot day consider packing a cool bag to keep any fruit or leaves fresh. One or two 'don'ts': don't pick beside a busy road (as much for the dust and petrol fumes on the crop as for the danger); or where chemical sprays might well have been used (e.g. right next to manicured public gardens); don't pick where many dogs are regularly walked (extra 'aromas' are not required, thanks); or where furious bulls reside; and never trespass.

This is just sensible stuff, and all that said, it's a joy to go out into the wild on a lovely day foraging for ingredients with which to make drinks. Dandelions, sloes, blackberries, elderflowers and elderberries, rosehips, nettles and oak leaves are out there for the taking – and all feature in recipes in this book. Take a picnic, your children, a good book and make a day of it!

# TIMING AND SEASONS

I strongly advise making drinks from ingredients that are properly in season. They'll taste fresher, 'truer', better all round if they have been grown according to their natural ripening season, with minimal intervention and sourced relatively near at hand – even if you are buying in the crops from a large shop rather than growing your own.

As for home-grown, seasonality is everything, of course, and you will want to swoop down on key ingredients at exactly the right moment: i.e. when ripe and ready, but before they turn the corner and go 'over'. It really pays to keep up with the neighbours here, swapping your gluts of fruit and veg. Or, if you are not a gardener, train a beady eye on nearby 'pick your own' farms as well as local veggie-box delivery schemes so you can get exactly the right natural ingredients quickly when the time is right, all tasting at their very best.

# Spring and summer cropping

The moment in spring for starting to make drinks from home-grown or wild ingredients is late April, when some of the flowers you might use have started to hit full bloom. Dandelions are the first of the lot. Tradition in England dictates that you pick them on 23 April, St George's Day, but only if it's sunny, I say. So, make Dandelion Wine (see page 46) in late April through May, and by then the first elderflowers should be ready, June being the main month for using these lovely blossoms (see pages 42–45).

Rhubarb is the first fresh fruit I ferment each year (see page 60), followed by the early summer crops of strawberries and gooseberries (see pages 56–7), although leave the latter to get ripe and pink if you want a rosé wine from it. Oak Leaf Wine can be made in early summer from young green leaves if you like, or wait until high summer for a more full-bodied, tannic white (see page 75).

Midsummer is unsurprisingly a season of great opportunities for a drinks-maker. Roses and lavender bushes bloom and the green herbs' heyday is followed by blackcurrants, redcurrants, raspberries, and more strawberries. Late summer sees the start of the apple and plum season and, in a hot year, blackberries are already starting to turn purple.

At the height of summer – July and August – many of us disappear for a week or two on holiday, sometimes leaving our most tempting fruit to the mercy of birds and wild animals, or, sadly, to turn ripe or rotten before they've been picked.

## SPRING AND SUMMER CROPS

| SPRING | SUMMER | | |
| --- | --- | --- | --- |
| Elderflowers | Blackberries | Mint | Rose petals |
| Dandelions | Blackcurrants | Nettles | Sage |
| Green gooseberries | Camomile | Oak leaves | Strawberries |
| Mint | Cherries | Pink gooseberries | Thyme |
| Nettles | Chillies | Plums | |
| Oak leaves | Cucumbers | Raspberries | |
| Rhubarb | Damsons | Redcurrants | |
| Rose petals | Lavender | Rhubarb | |

# Autumn and winter cropping

Autumn is a glorious time for drinks-making. It is apple-gathering season, of course, and pears are ripe, too. Both crops have a long ripening period, so there should be no huge rush to harvest and press. To check if an apple or pear is ready, pick the odd one from September onwards and cut into it; if the outside layer of the pips is still creamy-white, then the fruit is underripe. Brown pips mean a riper crop. Have several sessions of picking, pressing and drinks-making through the autumn if you have an abundant orchard harvest (see pages 92–101).

Blackberries can have a long season, too, often starting to ripen in the late summer but going strong through the autumn, depending on how much sun is shining on each bush. Again, expect to get several goes at 'brambling' over several weeks, though stop picking when berries grow slushy-squashy and cobwebs drape the bushes (see recipes on pages 66–9). Elderberries, grapes, damsons and quinces are all earlier autumn crops, while sloes and rosehips will be ready in late autumn and way after the first frosts (and sloes are improved for a natural freeze, see recipes on pages 76–7).

Winter doesn't bring much from nature's stores, although you can pull up the last parsnips for wine. This is the season for making drinks from store-cupboard and other 'timeless' ingredients, such as honey, eggs and spices (see pages 122–31).

## AUTUMN AND WINTER CROPS

| AUTUMN | Damsons | Quinces | WINTER |
|---|---|---|---|
| Apples | Elderberries | Raspberries | Parsnips |
| Blackberries | Grapes | Rosehips | Rosehips |
| Chillies | Pears | Sloes | |

# THE TEN ESSENTIAL BITS OF KIT

## 1. STERILIZING AND CLEANING EQUIPMENT

Buy a simple powder or tablets for sterilizing drinks-making equipment from a specialist brew shop. Use in solution to sterilize all equipment, including every type of container and airlocks, bungs, siphons, spoons, mashers and jugs, and always rinse well afterwards with loads of cold water. Make sure a long-handled bottle brush, washing-up liquid and plenty of new dishcloths and tea towels are on hand for cleaning.

## 2. PANS AND BUCKETS

A large metal preserving pan – preferably two – is essential for mashing up, macerating (soaking) and cooking fruit or vegetables. Some people use a simple plastic bucket on the floor for mashing or soaking, but I'm particular about this and use large stainless-steel pans at worktop level every time.

## 3. MEASURING JUGS

One large and one small plastic or glass jug with clear measurements on the side are crucial for drinks-making.

## 4. FUNNELS

You will need large and small funnels, including at least one with a narrow end small enough to fit into the neck of an ordinary wine bottle (or beer bottle). These can be used for adding powder as well as liquid ingredients.

## 5. SCALES

Make sure your scales are capable of weighing small amounts of powdered ingredients such as yeast or citric acid. Electronic scales are recommended.

## 6. MUSLIN BAGS AND SIEVES

You will need muslin cloths and/or fine sieves to strain your drinks. Muslin is best for wines, but fine sieves are more apt for tisanes or getting the pips out of cordials (you can even use a tea-strainer for a small quantity). I favour clean, new muslin bags, which are inexpensive and can go straight on the compost heap afterwards, together with the discarded fruit! You can make your own, of course, from muslin off-cuts, but the twentieth-century tradition of using old tights to strain drinks is, in my view, rather too unappealing.

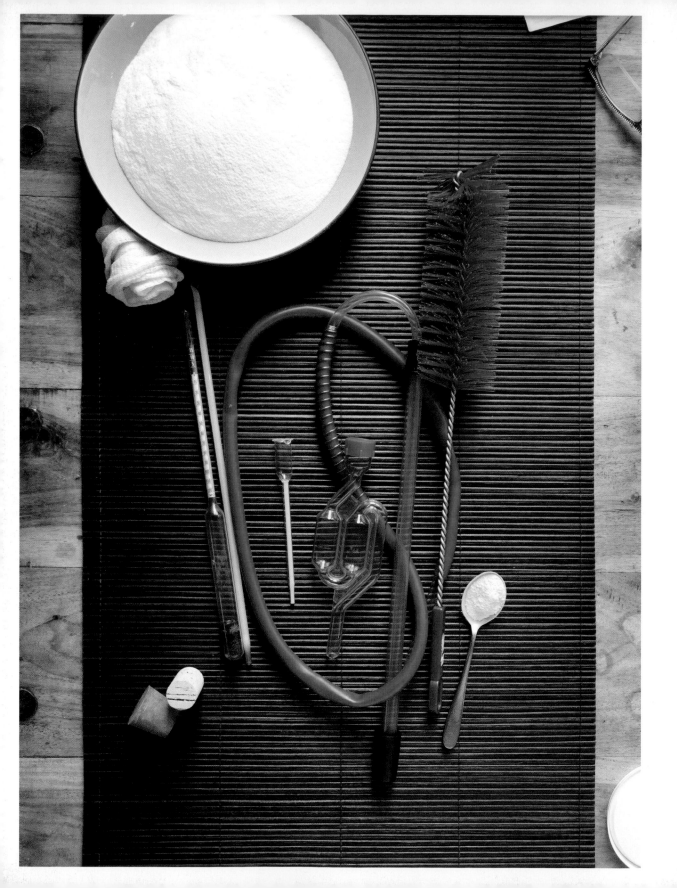

## 7. SIPHON

This is a long plastic tube that is used to move liquid from one container to another; useful when 'racking off' wine, mead or beer (taking the liquid off the yeast sediment; see page 30) and when bottling. Use by placing the second empty container or bottle at a lower height than the first, put one end of the siphon into the bottom of the liquid, and suck gently until gravity does the rest for you. Warning! It takes a little practice to get this right, and you need to have all the containers you want filled ready and waiting so you don't have to stop and start the process, messily.

## 8. DEMI-JOHNS

A demi-john is a 4.5 litre/8 pint (or 1 gallon) glass jar with a narrow top that fits a bung and airlock, and is the most common vessel used for fermentation by the small-scale amateur brewer. You can buy cheaper plastic versions but they're not nearly so attractive.

## 9. AIRLOCKS AND BUNGS

To keep bad bacteria and bugs out of the demi-john, fit a sterilized rubber bung with a hole in it for an airlock. The bung is usually rubber; the airlock can be glass or plastic (I favour plastic as glass airlocks break easily). Pour a little sterilized or cooled, boiled water into the airlock. The carbon dioxide bubbles up from your fermenting drink, yet no air can pass back into the vessel. Fit both components tightly.

## 10. THERMOMETER

Yeast will not work if the temperature of the liquid it's added to is too hot – in fact, it will die. Make sure your base drink is under 30°C/86°F to be on the safe side, using a long kitchen thermometer to test. Be aware it can take a hot liquid in a sunny kitchen many hours to cool down to under 30°C. Try to be patient; I learned this one the hard way, although you can always add more yeast down the line if you realize you've 'frazzled' the first lot!

## OTHER EQUIPMENT

Make you have some 'everyday' kitchen equipment easily to hand: teaspoons; tablespoons, or measures to the same amount; a good, solid potato masher for crushing fruit; sharp knives; a large grater (for ginger) and small nutmeg grater (for spices); a pestle and mortar; and a simple citrus-fruit squeezer may be handy (if you don't have the hands of a playground bully).

They're not crucial at first, but the super-keen drinks-maker might want to invest in other bits of kit, especially a hydrometer, which is used to estimate a liquid's alcohol level by measuring the density of the fluid. This is a little like a wide, heavy thermometer with levels written on the side. It is suspended in the fluid both before and after fermentation, and the last reading subtracted from the first gives an approximate idea of the alcohol level. Another handy gadget is a hand corking machine, which slots new corks into wine or beer bottles.

# Extra ingredients

## Sugar

The recipes in this book mainly use white sugar, but occasionally I've suggested using brown sugar in the tips that follow, for extra richness. Use ordinary, inexpensive granulated sugar whenever a liquid is hot or to be heated, as it will dissolve easily, but use caster and, best of all, brewer's fine powdered sugar when adding to cool fluid. The latter can be found in brewers' shops and on the internet.

## Yeast

Buy small amounts of yeast regularly from a specialist home-brew shop for making wine, cider and mead. I find wine yeast, sold all-in-one in a sachet with nutrient, suitable for most purposes – the nutrient is there to feed the yeast and help it along. Follow the instructions on your particular brand of yeast, bearing in mind you might need only a proportion of a large sachet for just one demi-john. Buy brewer's yeast for beer and baker's yeast for ginger beer. You can find out much more about the various yeast strains and the effect they have on fermenting drinks by reading specialist books and articles if preferred. Throw out unused old yeast, especially opened packets – it's inexpensive stuff.

## Citric acid and citrus fruit

Certain drinks need an extra refreshing tang added to balance out the flavours, in the form of citric acid (in powder form) or lemon juice and lemon rind. Buy fresh citric acid sachets from a home-brew shop or chemist, and stock up on fresh, ripe, unwaxed and preferably organic lemons. Citric acid is also a natural preservative.

## Pectic enzyme

A few drinks benefit from a pinch of pectic enzyme powder added to destroy the pectin and resulting cloudiness in the liquid. This is available from home-brew shops; I've indicated in one or two recipes when to use it.

## Base spirits

Do buy decent-quality base spirits at all times. These don't need to be premium vodkas or gins, but relatively inexpensive brands from a reliable shop. See page 122 for more advice.

# MAKING, STORING AND AGEING

Some of the drinks in this book, such as teas and cordials, are easy enough, but it helps to get more of a low-down on those that involve fermentation.

## Fermenting and infusing

Keep any drinks that are fermenting or infusing in a cool, dark place – but not too cold in the case of fermentation, or the process will slow down to a frustrating snail's pace. You can see how fast your drink is fermenting by watching the bubbles in the airlock: expect at least four bubbles a minute, even more when the yeast is working at its hardest.

Demi-johns can sit in any coolish, shady corner inside the house, but make sure they are kept well out of the sun. In winter, fermentation tends to be quieter. To speed things up, simply move the fermenting drink to a warmer room. And if you are worried about losing the colour of a prettily hued wine or other liquid, especially pink drinks, consider making it in brown-glass demi-johns, as this should stop the colour fading as fast.

## Racking off

It's important to 'rack off' a fermenting drink properly in order to remove the dead yeast sediment (or 'lees'). The siphon method is explained on page 27. Where a wine or beer has thrown a lot of sediment, you might need to go through this process more than once before bottling. You can buy stabilizing powders from home-brew shops if you want to bring fermentation to a halt earlier than nature would to create a crisp, neutral style, and fining (clarifying) powders can be added to help settle fine particles in a very cloudy liquid. I prefer to keep intervention to a minimum, however.

## To age or not to age your wine

Don't be afraid to keep/age your wine in the demi-johns after fermentation has finished, before or after racking off, as you wish. It can mature here very well, and I have found this (rather than early bottling) useful in the case of wines such as Oak Leaf Wine and Parsnip Wine (see pages 75 and 105). Conversely, if you want a youthful, bright, crisp style of wine, make sure it ferments relatively quickly in a warm room, and consider stabilizing it after a few weeks to stop further fermentation, then bottle and drink it quickly.

## How to keep drinks

Once your drinks are bottled, keep wines and spirits as you would do shop-bought ones: in a cool, dark place, resting on their sides if a cork is used, or in the refrigerator or freezer in the case of cordials. Once opened, light wines will last at least three days if resealed and stored in a cool spot, while opened cordials, liqueurs and spirit infusions should keep several weeks.

# TROUBLESHOOTING

The recipes in this book are refreshingly easy and straightforward. But there can be problems with drinks that involve fermentation. Here are some of the common conundrums, and how to resolve them without fuss:

| Problem | Solution |
|---|---|
| Fermentation doesn't start at all | You may have killed the yeast by putting it in liquid that was too hot, or perhaps you are using old yeast. Make sure you have fresh stock and simply add the same quantity to the liquid again, removing the bung for a very short time only. |
| Fermentation starts but stops far too early | This often happens in winter when jars are stored in a cold room. Move the fermentation vessel to a warmer place. |
| Fermentation is fast and furious, leading to liquid bubbling back through the airlock and spilling down the sides | This isn't a disaster, and should only last a short time. However, you'll need to clean the airlock and bung and replace regularly while it's happening. And mop up! Or consider using a 'bung' of cotton wool for a few days during the first vigorous fermentation, replacing the cotton wool with the airlock and bung after things settle down. |
| The water in the airlock turns black | Take the airlock out, covering the hole in the bung with a napkin. Empty, wash and sterilize the airlock thoroughly, fill with fresh water and replace as quickly as possible. The 'bad' water should not have gone into your fermenting liquid so don't worry. (You may wish to use water with a little sterilizing powder dissolved in it if this happens a lot.) |
| The finished drink tastes synthetic, and slightly chemically | You may not have rinsed all the sterilizing solution off your bottles or stoppers before using them. Always be most careful to rinse anything that has been sterilized. Another cause might be overuse of stabilizer (see page 30), which some people consider can give a slightly 'concrete' taste to wine. Consider dropping this practice and, next time, waiting until a wine stops fermenting naturally. |
| After bottling, the wine tastes and smells 'musty', like damp cardboard | I'll bet you're using natural cork stoppers! The wine is 'corked' – in other words, it has been affected by a taint created by the cork bark. Make sure you sterilize and rinse corks thoroughly before use, or switch to screw-caps or flip-top bottles instead. (I don't recommend synthetic corks, as they are difficult to get in and out of bottles.) |

# BOTTLES

You can use brown or green bottles, but I prefer clear ones, so that I can see the attractive glints of light and colour in the finished drink. Of course, it's entirely up to you whether to use old glass wine bottles with screw-caps or corks, flip-top beer or ginger ale-type bottles, or plastic containers for bottling your drinks. But there are three things to bear in mind

1. Make sure the container and lid is squeaky clean and sterilized.

2. Never transfer liquid that is still fermenting into closed containers unless you are quite sure they are strong enough to withstand the pressure of the gas.

3. Fermenting liquids with lids closed tight can cause plastic and glass bottles to explode very suddenly indeed. Loosen and reclose the tops of such liquids from time to time, turning your face away when you do so to avoid possible injury.

# A NOTE ON FILLING UP

Do be careful to top up any demi-johns when you start the fermentation process. They should be filled to just under the neck and may need topping up with cold, boiled water at the beginning as the liquid produced may fall short after the boiling, reducing or macerating processes. Conversely, make sure you leave some space in containers filled with homemade drinks to be frozen, as the fluid will expand a little when it grows icy.

# GIVING DRINKS AS GIFTS

It's oh-so-easy to grab a bottle from a shop to give as a birthday present or take to a party, but how much more impressive to bring along a drink you actually made yourself? Homemade drinks are up there with homemade truffles or jams, in my view. Actually, they are a lot more fun than jam, come to think of it!

It's a good idea to put your drinks into attractive bottles and jars, though, so do save any handsome glass containers that come your way, washing and sterilizing them thoroughly before pouring your precious concoctions into them with a funnel. Particular styles of wine come in unusual, appealing bottles – for example, certain sweet French Muscats or Provençal rosés – so look out for 'empties'. Kilner jars used to make drinks are also nice to give away, especially in the case of spirit infusions and liqueurs.

If the drink has 'solids' in it, such as lemon peel, cinnamon, blackberries or lavender, take a long hard look at it and see if these need taking out, or replacing with just a small fresh piece or a few new berries purely for visual appeal. In short, does it actually look attractive? If not, and the drink has finished fermenting, strain off the solids and decant the drink into a fresh bottle.

# JAZZ UP YOUR HOMEMADE DRINKS

❋ Use classic brown or cream luggage labels/swing tags around the necks of bottles and jars to identify the drinks inside, or to add a personal message. And decorate the labels with simple coloured borders.

❋ Cut up squares of felt or pieces of chic vintage material, as well as coloured paper and card to make tops and simple 'jackets' for bottles and jars.

❋ Write with metallic pens on glass or labels – and if your handwriting is as scruffy as mine, get someone else to do the calligraphy!

❋ Use rubber stamps or festive stencils for creative printing on labels.

❋ Tie little extras, such as cinnamon sticks, or lavender heads, or small, dried chillies – anything you like – to the outside of bottles, securing tightly with natural string, raffia, or ribbons.

❋ Pack bottles into interesting basket-ware, drinks holders, small hampers, or hat boxes, and tie silk or velvet ribbons around to complete the gift wrap.

# FLORAL DRINKS

Making drinks out of flowers sounds like something a child would do – pounding up Granny's dahlias to make her a nice cup of tea is reasonable when you are four. But there are some genuinely tempting drinks to be made from certain blooms, both wild and cultivated. Admittedly, the repertoire is somewhat limited, as only a few flowers can be used, but happily those that can are commonly found. Who doesn't have access to roses, lavender or (far too many) dandelions?

Several senses will revel in these drinks; not only are they visually stimulating and attractive while gathering, making and on completion, but they each have quite a beguiling perfume. Oh, and they taste good, too. Aim to pick flowers on sunny, dry days, and go for healthy, clean heads in full bloom, avoiding any browning petals. Only gather flowers very close to the time you will use them, as they don't keep well.

# Elderflower Cordial

*Makes just over
2 litres (3½ pints)*

*Keeps for 1 month
in the refrigerator*

How beautifully the sight of delicate, frothy white elderflower blossoms and their sappy, sweet scent conjures up the month of June! I used to make this cordial in small quantities and drink it for only a few weeks each year; now I freeze plenty to ensure that a whiff of early summer is possible throughout the year. I have tried a few versions but this is my favourite.

**1.8kg (4lb) sugar**
**1.8 litres (3 pints) very hot water**
**25 elderflower sprays**
**1 tbsp citric acid (see page 29)**
**3 limes**
**1 lemon**

1. Put the sugar into a preserving pan and pour on the hot water, stirring until the sugar is dissolved. Cool for 20 minutes.
2. Meantime, shake the flower heads over the sink to remove any dust or insects, then swish them gently in a bowl of cool water. Strain and shake until semi-dry.
3. Using small sharp scissors, carefully snip off all the main stalks and as many of the medium-sized ones as you have time to do, leaving only the floral sprigs.
4. Push the flowers down into the warm sugar syrup and add the citric acid. Stir.
5. Pare one-third of the thin outer rind from the fruit and add to the pan, then slice the semi-peeled fruit and add it, too.
6. Stir everything together, cover tightly and keep in a cool, dark place for 24 hours.
7. Strain through muslin into a clean pan and bottle.

* *Freezes well in small plastic drinks bottles – don't fill completely when freezing though; leave some room for the frozen liquid to expand.*

* *Be careful when opening older bottles of cordial, as they may have started to ferment. To avoid this, keep them very cold, drink up quickly or freeze until needed.*

* *Make up the cordial with sparkling as well as still water.*

* *I think the perfumed nature of limes works effectively; you can of course substitute lemons, using fewer, as they tend to be larger and sharper.*

* *Add peeled, thickly grated root ginger (6cm/2½in in size) at the same stage as you dissolve the sugar, to add a subtle peppery, earthy note to the cordial.*

* *Combine the finished cordial with chilled dry (brut) sparkling wine for a simple but wonderful aperitif – cava works particularly well as it is fairly neutral.*

* *Make elderflower cocktails with cordial and gin or vodka, plus a splash of lemon or lime juice. I always add a sprig of lightly bruised fresh mint.*

# Elderflower 'Champagne'

*Makes 4 litres*
*(7 pints)*

*Best enjoyed fresh,*
*but will keep for*
*several weeks stored*
*in a cool, dark place*

A mildly alcoholic, softly spritzy wine that's a doddle to make – though see the 'warning' below! Elderflowers should have enough natural yeast on them to create the fizz without any additions, though you can add a pinch of dried yeast if fermentation doesn't start spontaneously.

This is a similar process to making cordial, but here the liquid is allowed to ferment. For that to happen you must not kill the natural yeast on the flowers by plunging them into hot sugar syrup, hence using cold water here.

Warning! The fizz in this 'Champagne' is highly unpredictable and varies from crop to crop. Be very careful to use strong bottles, preferably flip-top, thick glass ones. And open with caution. Check stored bottles regularly and release gas as a precaution from time to time, especially if you have used extra yeast.

**25 elderflower sprays**
**2 lemons**
**500g (1lb) caster sugar**
**1½ tbsp white wine vinegar**
**4 litres (7 pints) cold water**
**pinch of dried yeast (optional, see above)**

1. Shake the elderflower heads well to remove any insects and then cut off the major stalks. Do not wash them. Put in a very clean bucket, and add the thin outer rind of the lemons, then their juice.
2. Add the caster sugar, vinegar and cold water and stir until the sugar is dissolved.
3. Cover tightly with muslin or tea towels and leave for several days – but check every day to see if fermentation has started. If it has not after 3 days or so, add a pinch of dried yeast, stir and wait a little longer. Bottle.

* *This drink is slightly cloudy, and will throw a sediment with time. This sediment is harmless, but you might want to discard any from the bottom of the bottle.*
* *Lemons work better than limes in this recipe – increase the amount of fruit used for a sharper tang if desired.*
* *Serve this with a light lunch of undressed leafy salad, mild goats' cheese and fresh tomatoes.*

# Elderflower Wine

*Makes 4.5 litres
(8 pints)*

*Will keep for
1–2 years.*

I must confess I've only made this once or twice, as I adore the Cordial and 'Champagne' so much. Not to mention my leaving some blooms to turn into berries (see Elderberry Wine, page 70). So there aren't usually many elderflowers left … However, some people absolutely love this, and it is an appealing, light, Muscatty wine.

**approximately 600ml (1 pint) elderflowers, after stems cut off,
  lightly pressed into a jug
4.5 litres (8 pints) boiling water
1.3kg (3lb) sugar
2 lemons
yeast and nutrient, according to the packet (see page 29)**

1. Place the elderflowers in a large preserving pan, and pour on the just-boiled water.
2. Add the sugar, grated rind and juice of the lemons. Stir well.
3. Cool until under 30°C (86°F), then add the yeast and nutrient.
4. Cover tightly with muslin and leave to ferment somewhere warm for 4 days.
5. Strain through muslin into a sterilized demi-john, put in a bung and airlock and leave to ferment. When the fermentation has finished and the wine is clear, rack off the lees (see page 30) into a second sterilized demi-john and leave for 6 weeks. Then rack again, and bottle.

\* *Elderflower Wine must always be served cool, and makes an aromatic, refreshing aperitif, rather like a light French or Italian white wine.*

\* *Try matching this wine with white fish or seafood dishes.*

# Dandelion Wine

*Makes 4.5 litres*
*(8 pints)*

*Drink within*
*3 months of bottling*

This is often the first wine to be made each spring from fresh ingredients. Tradition dictates picking on St George's Day, 23 April, but I've made Dandelion Wine earlier, and into the first half of May. One of my neighbours makes a rich, dark, long-aged version of this wine by using the full heads of dandelions and keeping it in demi-johns for years, but this is my quite different take – using the petals only to make a light, pale, dry white for early drinking. It tastes like a simple but refreshing Italian Soave or Frascati.

**2 litres (3½ pints) dandelion petals**
**4.5 litres (8 pints) boiling water**
**1 orange**
**2 lemons**
**1kg (2lb 4oz) fine sugar, preferably brewer's sugar (see page 29)**
**yeast and nutrient, according to packet (see page 29)**

1. Pick 2 large plastic bags full of dandelions, cutting them just below the head. Sort through, and shake to remove any insects. Now for the fiddly, sticky bit: using sharp scissors, cut away the green sappy part of each head, leaving only the petals and a little bit of the white inner head. Do this until you have 2 litres' (3½ pints') worth of petals, when packed lightly into a measuring jug.
2. Put the flowers into a preserving pan or clean bucket. Pour the boiling water over them, then add the rind of the orange and lemons. Stir, cover and leave for 4 hours to steep.
3. Add the sugar and the juice of the fruit and stir until the sugar dissolves.
4. Cool to under 30°C (86°F), then strain through a fine muslin bag into another pan, squeezing the bag to get as much flavour out as possible.
5. Add yeast and nutrient to the liquid and pour into a sterilized demi-john; put in a bung and airlock and leave to ferment out over several weeks, then rack off (see page 30) and bottle.

* *Dandelions have a sticky sap that stains the skin – use thin plastic gloves when cutting off the petals.*
* *This wine is light, dry and delicate, and a good summer white – serve well chilled as a perfect partner for salads, tomatoes, white fish and prawns.*

# Rose Petal Drink

*Makes 2 litres
(3 ½ pints)*

The scent and colour of rose petals can be rather elusive when making drinks. I favour 'soft' rose drinks over fermented, as I think they capture the essence of the fresh flower best – delicate and lightly perfumed and unmistakably made from this wonderful flower. This recipe comes from Azerbaijan. Make it with dark-red petals to get a lovely rich colour.

*Enjoy on the day
it is made, as it
does not keep well
and the fragrance
is soon lost*

**petals from 4–5 large roses**
**2 litres (3½ pints) water**
**splash of lemon juice, approximately 10ml (to taste)**
**3 tbsp caster sugar**

1. Rinse the rose petals gently and dry on kitchen paper.
2. Bring the water to boiling point in a large pan, then turn off the heat and add the petals and lemon juice. Stir.
3. Let it stand for 6–8 hours. Strain and discard the petals.
4. Add the sugar and stir until dissolved. (Heat the liquid just a little bit if sugar does not dissolve easily.) Stir and chill.
5. Serve this in a clear glass jug to show off the lovely colour. Add ice and float a few petals on the surface to garnish.

* *This delicate drink will be overwhelmed by rich or over-sweet food, but small, light savoury snacks (especially meze dishes) or elegant, simple cakes and biscuits work well with it.*

* *Be absolutely sure only to use unsprayed rose petals. Even after washing, petals that have been sprayed with pesticide might harbour nasty residues. Never use shop-bought roses for the same reason. You can use wild hedgerow rose petals, but as these are smaller you need a lot of them! And they tend to have a lighter perfume than cultivated garden roses.*

* *Damask roses are the variety that give the strongest perfume to drinks.*

* *Try a simple tea version by covering petals from 8–10 large roses with 1 litre (1¾ pints) of water and bring slowly to the boil. Simmer for a few minutes, strain into 6 teacups and add honey to taste.*

# Lavender Lemonade

*Makes 1.5 litres*
*(2½ pints)*

*Store in the fridge*
*and drink within*
*a day or so – this*
*is best made in*
*small quantities*

This soft drink is one of my firm favourites. It's easy, quick, impressive – and kids love it, too. The first time I made it, I was bewitched by the lovely fragrance of steeped lavender that stole through the house. And by the fact the liquid turns pink only when you add the lemons (why, I couldn't say). Make it from flowers that have 'turned the corner' (semi-dry) in high summer, or from dried blooms whenever you like.

**15g (½oz) lavender heads**
**500ml (18fl oz) boiling water**
**150g (5½oz) sugar**
**1.2 litres (2 pints) cold water**
**5 ripe lemons**

1. Shake the lavender gently to remove any insects.
2. Put the flower heads into a saucepan and pour over the boiling water. Bring to the boil again and simmer for a minute or two.
3. Turn the heat off and leave for 10 minutes to steep. Strain.
4. Add the sugar and stir to dissolve. Add the cold water.
5. Squeeze the lemons directly into the pan – watch it turn pink! – then strain again if you want rid of any lemon pips and pith.
6. Taste to see how concentrated the flavour is – and when serving, add more water to dilute according to taste.

✳ *Serve in a clear glass jug to make the most of the pretty colour. Add plenty of ice and stir with thick dried lavender stalks for effect.*

✳ *This is an immensely refreshing hot-weather drink, especially on a heavy, humid late-summer's day, al fresco.*

✳ *Add a shot of vodka for a great instant cocktail. Even better, mix lavender lemonade and vodka in a cocktail shaker with ice cubes, shake and strain into martini glasses for an elegant scented aperitif.*

# Lavender Vodka

*Makes 700ml*
*(1¼ pints)*

*At its best within*
*a couple of weeks*
*of making*

As easy as it gets. Again, the distinctive scent of lavender appears quickly and is retained well in the spirit. But you must remove the lavender stalks after two weeks; otherwise the vodka turns brown and starts to taste woody – not good!

**15–20 dried lavender flower heads, long stalks still attached**
**70cl good-quality vodka (unflavoured)**

1. Don't wash the lavender, but do shake it gently to remove any insects.
2. Now simply pour a little vodka into a jug and set aside, then push the lavender stalks down into the bottle, head first.
3. Top up with the reserved vodka (keeping any little amount leftover in a jam jar for topping up later), seal again and turn several times.
4. Turn every day or so for 14 days, then take lid off and check. The liquid should have a lovely floral scent. Remove the lavender. Top up with more reserved vodka, reseal and store in a cool, dark place.

* *Serve ice cold in shot glasses in hot weather.*
* *Consider making in half-bottle quantities using 8–9 lavender stalks, as a full bottle might be too much to drink quickly! This vodka doesn't last as well as some spirit infusions (see also pages 122–31).*
* *This is a 'dry' vodka, which works best in my view, though you could always make a sweet version by adding sugar (approximately 3–4 tsp) at the initial steeping stage if you like.*
* *Serve with fruity, cool desserts such as sorbets, granitas or rosewater panna cotta.*

# SUMMER FRUIT DRINKS

I love the plump, juicy fruit of summer just as much for making into drinks as for eating. In a good year, fruits such as blackcurrants, gooseberries and plums can produce a sudden and sensational glut, so I welcome as many ideas as possible for using them up. Here's a wide-ranging selection of drinks to make from the high-summer harvests, including soft fruit cordial for all the family and some tempting wines.

Summer, as we all know, often doesn't last long and I miss these crops when it's over every year. For ideas on making these drinks out of season (and why not?) from frozen, tinned or shop-bought fruit, see page 14.

# Blackcurrant Cordial

*Makes approx.*
*750ml (1¼ pints)*

*Keeps well in the*
*refrigerator for*
*up to 6 weeks*

It's amazing how expensive shop-bought blackcurrants are – far better to grow your own, or beg from a friend or neighbour who has a wonderful glut. Blackcurrants seem to need picking all at once, and in a rush before the birds get them. So do try this vitamin-C-packed cordial, which children love.

Wear an old apron and plastic gloves while attempting to make blackcurrant cordial if you don't want to end up with purple clothes and fingers. It's hard to imagine anyone taking a dislike to this drink, so make plenty to last you through the year (see freezing tip below).

**800g (1lb 12oz) blackcurrants**
**500g (1lb 2oz) caster sugar**
**500ml (18fl oz) water**
**juice of 2 lemons**

1. Work through the blackcurrants, destalking as many as possible. (You don't need to 'top' them or to be quite as fussy about the tiny stalks as you are when preparing them to eat, thank goodness). Wash them well.
2. Place the fruit, sugar and water in a large saucepan and heat up slowly and gently, stirring to dissolve the sugar.
3. Bring the pan to a very gentle simmer for 5 minutes only. Do not boil vigorously or for any longer, or the fresh taste of the fruit might be lost. It's not supposed to turn into jam!
4. Add the lemon juice, stirring well. Simmer gently for another 5 minutes, turn off the heat, cover and leave.
5. Once cool, either sieve twice or pass through a fine muslin. Pour into sterilized bottles.

* *This freezes well, so I always split up the batch into several small plastic bottles and freeze some. Leave a bit of space at the top of each bottle you intend to freeze, as the liquid expands on freezing.*
* *Freeze the cordial as individual ice cubes and pop into glasses of cold water to keep kids happily hydrated in summer.*
* *Experiment with different variations on this theme: for example, use this recipe but replace some blackcurrants with 30 per cent raspberries or redcurrants, or a mix of 15 per cent of each.*
* *Mix with ginger ale for a fun, fizzy, slightly peppery long drink.*
* *Make up with sparkling water and a lime slice for kids' mocktails, or splash into cold dry sparkling wine for a less powerful version of Kir Royale for grown-ups.*
* *Reduce the cordial further to make a lovely sauce for game and duck, or to pour over sorbet, ice cream, cheesecakes and meringues.*

# Strawberry Wine

*Makes 4.5 litres*
*(8 pints)*

*Store in a cool,*
*dark place*

*Best at about*
*4–6 months*

Ahh, strawberries. Their scent and juicy flesh are so redolent of summer days that I don't blame anyone for thinking they would rather simply eat fresh strawberries and never cook or preserve them, let alone make wine from them. But then I would tell them that strawberry wine is a very wonderful drink. It's so easy, and as that unmistakeable sweet perfume rises and the bright-red froth foams, it becomes a joy to make.

A delectable, salmon-pink rosé hue, it delivers all the natural flavour of this glorious fruit. My latest batch was slightly off-dry, juicy and moreish, yet with crisp acidity to balance it. After months of fermenting and ageing, the wine continues to give off the tempting aroma of the fresh fruit. This is one of the very best fruit wines. A waste of good berries? No way!

**4 litres (7 pints) boiling water**
**1.8kg (4lb) strawberries, preferably local**
**900g (2lb) sugar**
**½ tbsp critic acid**
**yeast and nutrient, according to the packet (see page 29)**
**2 lemons**

1. Bring the water to boiling point in a large preserving pan. Meanwhile, wash and roughly hull the strawberries. Add the fruit to the boiling water and simmer for 10 minutes. Stir, but be careful not to mash up the berries.
2. Turn off the heat, add the sugar, citric acid, yeast and nutrient, and pared rind and juice of the lemons. Stir, cover securely (strawberry juice attracts flies!) and leave overnight to steep and cool.
3. The next day, strain into a sterilized demi-john, add the yeast and fit an airlock and bung. Rest the demi-john in a bucket or the bath in case it froths over.
4. After fermentation, which is likely to be vigorous and relatively quick (especially in hot weather), rack off (see page 30) and bottle.

* *Store in a dark place if you want to retain the pink colour. You might consider using a dark glass demi-john and eventually dark glass bottles, though the latter does seem a shame when pink wine looks so pretty.*

* *This isn't a wine to keep for too long, or the fresh, fruity aroma and flavour will start to fade. Wine made in July is rewarded by a cool glass in November – a welcome memory of summer on a dark, cold night.*

* *This is not properly sweet wine so don't drink it with a rich dessert. Its off-dry flavour and juicy qualities work well with a crisp, fresh fruit salad.*

# Gooseberry Wine

*Makes 4.5 litres
(8 pints)*

*Keeps best in the
refrigerator, for
up to a year*

Use this recipe with gooseberries of any hue. It makes a superb fruit wine, with good crisp acidity and plenty of bright, fruity aroma and flavour to balance it out. During an exceptionally hot early summer one year, I ended up with a glut of especially ripe, bright cerise gooseberries. Six months later, the resulting wine was even more tasty, and the candy-pink colour added extra appeal.

Pink gooseberry wine at six months old is like a dry, refreshing, young European rosé; it develops into a delightfully refreshing, elegant, dry rosé almost Provençal in style. Green gooseberry wine is more akin to a light, dry French white.

Note: you don't need citric acid or lemons here – gooseberries are quite sour enough, although the end result is surprisingly well balanced. In my opinion this is one of the most successful of the fruit wines.

**1.8kg (4lb) gooseberries, preferably very ripe and pink**
**pinch of pectic enzyme (see page 29)**
**yeast and nutrient, according to the packet (see page 29)**
**4.5 litres (8 pints) cold water**
**1.3kg (3lb) brewer's sugar (see page 29)**

1. Top and tail the gooseberries and wash them well. Place the fruit in a large, clean pan or bucket and mash with a potato masher. Add the enzyme, yeast and nutrient, and stir.
2. Pour the cold water over the mashed fruit, stir and cover loosely but well with clean linen.
3. Leave to stand for 3 days, stirring occasionally.
4. Strain through muslin into another clean container, add the sugar and stir well until completely dissolved.
5. Pour into a sterilized demi-john and fit an airlock and bung.
6. After fermentation – probably long and slow – leave to age in the demi-john for several more weeks, then rack off the small amount of sediment and bottle (see page 34).

* *Discard the solid parts of gooseberry after straining as they will have traces of yeast, nutrient and enzyme on them so can't be used in cooking.*
* *Try this wine with simple white fish or trout, as its delicate flavour matches them well.*

# Plum Wine

*Makes 4.5 litres*
*(8 pints)*

*Keeps for up to a year*

Plums can often seem like a precious commodity, especially if you are paying for decent shop-bought ones. But if you have plum trees a glut occurs almost annually, and it's quite a task to harvest all the plums before they become inedible windfalls – bruised and attracting wasps. Wine might be a welcome solution. This makes a really appealing, bright cerise, fresh and fruity rosé, much in the style of a dry French or Spanish pink. I make it with Victoria plums, but there's nothing to prevent you using other varieties of this lovely juicy fruit.

**2.2kg (5lb) ripe plums**
**4.5 litres (8 pints) water**
**pectic enzyme, according to the packet (see page 29)**
**1.5kg (3lb 5oz) sugar**
**yeast and nutrient, according to the packet (see page 29)**

1. Wash the plums and discard the bad parts of any that are rotten, split or mouldy.
2. Cut them into large pieces, retaining the stones, place in a large clean container and bruise them well with a potato masher or the back of a large metal spoon.
3. Boil 2 litres (3½ pints) of the water and pour over the crushed plum pieces, cover well and leave for several hours to steep.
4. Now add the rest of the cold water, and the enzyme. Cover again and leave to macerate for 3 days.
5. Strain through muslin into a preserving pan and heat up gently, adding the sugar and stirring until it dissolves (you shouldn't have to boil it).
6. Allow this liquor to cool to under 30°C (86°F), then add the yeast and nutrient.
7. Pour into a sterilized demi-john, and fit a bung and airlock. After fermentation you might need to rack this wine more than once to get rid of all the sediment (see page 30).

∗ *Drink this wine on its own, lightly chilled, or it's delicious with cold meats, especially chicken, turkey and pork, or mild cheeses.*

∗ *Remove the stones from the leftover plum pieces, and use the latter in myriad ways:*
   * *mulled plum jam, using red wine, port, spices and citrus peel*
   * *other preserves or chutneys*
   * *fruit compotes*
   * *fruit cakes*

# Rhubarb Wine

*Makes 4.5 litres*
*(8 pints)*

*Drink up within*
*6 months*

Some homemade wines, however good, don't taste especially strongly of the fruit used to make them. But this one does. So if you don't like rhubarb, be warned! I love rhubarb and always have a glut of it in early summer. Once the freezer is crammed with the chopped stalks, I make a demi-john or two of this wine, which has a distinctive, very light spritz after bottling for the first few months. Expect quite high acidity – a welcome, refreshing quality in my opinion – and a slightly earthy, apple-core quality (a bit like cava).

**1.3kg (3lb) rhubarb**
**4.5 litres (8 pints) boiling water**
**1.3kg (3lb) sugar**
**1 lemon**
**yeast and nutrient, according to the packet (see page 29)**

1. Cut the rhubarb into pieces approximately 3–5cm (1¼–2in) long, discarding the stumpy roots and very green tops of each stalk. Wash the pieces thoroughly.
2. Put the fruit in a large preserving pan or clean bucket and pour all the boiling water over it. Don't heat it up again; just stir and allow to steep for 20–30 minutes, by which time the stalks should have softened.
3. Press and bruise the fruit in the liquid using a potato masher or the back of a large metal spoon – you are aiming to squash it and extract plenty of juice. Keep mashing until the liquid is stained pink and the rhubarb is crushed a little, but not pulped.
4. Add the sugar and the pared peel and juice of the lemon. Stir well, cover loosely and leave to cool overnight.
5. Strain through fine muslin into a sterilized demi-john, adding the yeast and nutrient. Fit a bung and airlock.
6. After fermentation, rack off and bottle (see pages 30 and 34).

* *A delicious wine for late summer, this makes a great, palate-cleansing aperitif.*
* *This is a perfect base for homemade Kir, mixed with Crème de Cassis or Blackcurrant Cordial (see pages 62 or 54), as it has the high acid kick required to offset the sweet cassis.*
* *Use the rhubarb and lemon left in the muslin to make preserves, or add a little to a pan of stewed rhubarb for extra concentration and flavour. Remember: it is already sweetened.*
* *Serve the wine with seafood, especially cold prawns, crab and lobster.*

# Raspberry Gin

*Makes 1 litre
(1¾ pints)*

*Will keep and
improves with age
(see tip below)*

A splendid, aromatic gin infusion – and one that is vastly better if you take on board all the tips given below. Most important, use good-quality, medium-ripe fruit, and no pale or green berries, overripe or bruised ones. Remember that raspberries are at their best for only a day or two, so pick or buy and use quickly and with care.

**200g (7oz) raspberries**
**175g (6oz) sugar**
**1 litre (1¾ pints) gin**

1. Wash the raspberries thoroughly just before using; dry as much as possible and discard any damaged fruit.
2. Place the fruit in a 1-litre (1¾ pint) kilner jar and sprinkle the sugar on top. Fill the jar right up with the gin.
3. Seal and shake gently until the sugar is nearly dissolved and then store for several weeks, turning every now and then. Keep in a dark cupboard and drink only after 10 weeks.

* *Raspberry Gin improves with age, so 'cellar' some for a year or two, if you have the patience, noting any changes and the optimum stage for drinking your version.*

* *It's a good idea to keep it somewhere dark, as this helps retain the pretty deep-pink colour of the spirit.*

* *Raspberry Gin should be somewhat sweet, not cloying, and have a fresh aroma. When you first taste it, add a little more sugar if you think the infusion needs it. It's a good idea to taste after a few weeks to measure this, and you can add a little more gin to top it up at this stage.*

* *Shake in a cocktail shaker with a dash of dry vermouth, a splash of plain gin and plenty of ice, then strain into a martini glass for a mouthwatering summer cocktail.*

# Crème de Cassis

*Makes approximately*
*2½ litres (4½ pints)*

*Best enjoyed after*
*12 months maturing,*
*stored in a cool,*
*dark place*

For such a highly regarded, stylish drink, Crème de Cassis is surprisingly easy to make, provided you use decent red wine. Many beautiful cassis concoctions have been ruined by the addition of a rough bottle of red, or old, oxidized wine, so make sure you open fresh bottles for this job. Ripe, fruity reds are best – California Merlot or (red) Zinfandel, or southern French Grenache.

Note: this recipe is very similar to that for Crème de Mure on page 68 – but the Cassis is more acidic, with a tangy fresh lift to the finish.

**1.5kg (3lb 5oz) blackcurrants**
**2 litres (3½ pints) red wine**
**1.5kg (3lb 5oz) sugar, possibly more to taste**
**70cl vodka (unflavoured)**

1. Wash the blackcurrants well, then work through them using a pair of small, sharp scissors, cutting off any 'tufty' tops and stems. Place them in a large preserving pan and crush with a potato masher until all the berries burst and there's plenty of juice.
2. Pour the red wine over the top and stir well. Cover and leave to steep for 48 hours, stirring from time to time and covering again.
3. Strain through a muslin bag into a sterilized container. This can take some time, so consider hanging up the bag overnight, perhaps on the back of a chair, with the container underneath. Squeeze the bag at the end to get the last of the liquid out (wearing plastic gloves!).
4. Rinse the original pan and pour the juice back in, now adding the sugar. Stir well. Heat up gently, still stirring, until the sugar has dissolved and the liquid is very hot but not quite boiling. Leave at just under simmering point to reduce until the liquid thickens and turns slightly more syrupy. This may take an hour or more. Stir from time to time.
5. Taste your liqueur, adding more sugar if you think it needs it for flavour and texture and stirring the sugar to dissolve if so. Leave to cool.
6. Add in the spirit, stir well and pour into sterilized bottles.

* *Crème de Cassis also creates two traditional party classics – Kir and Kir Royale.*
  * *For a classic Kir: splash a small amount of Crème de Cassis in the bottom of a wine glass and top up with cold Aligoté (a grape from Burgundy) white wine, or use another dry, unoaked white – such as Muscadet.*
  * *For Kir Royale: splash 15ml (½ fl oz) Crème de Cassis into the bottom of a tall Champagne flute, then top up with chilled dry fizz, preferably Crémant de Bourgogne or even Champagne if you're feeling flash.*
* *Make a luxurious sauce for roast duck or goose with poultry stock, blackcurrants and a knob of butter, adding a spoonful or two of Crème de Cassis and heating through.*
* *Follow the French lead and pour Crème de Cassis on to ripe melons, or spoon over poached pears served with vanilla ice cream.*

# WILD DRINKS

This is my very favourite part of the book, to be honest. It gets
to the heart of why I started making my own drinks. Every autumn
I saw an abundance of wild fruit, covering the hedgerows, bushes
and trees, yet aside from the obvious trips to collect brambles for
puddings and jams, I couldn't think what to do with any of it. Now
I know, and not only for blackberries – versatile little gems though
they are – but rosehips, sloes, the damsons that grow in our field,
even certain leaves and weeds.

So here's a good range of drinks made from a wild harvest. Sure,
certain ingredients come and go – the birds get a crop of brambles,
or the best hedgerow for rosehips disappears, or a patch of land
is claimed for an arable crop instead of wild sloe bushes. But there's
bound to be something you can collect for drinks simply by making
a short walk from your front door (if you live in the countryside),
or by planning a longer day out foraging (if you live in a city).
It will be well worth it. And did I mention 'free'?

# Blackberry Cordial

Blackberry cordial works perfectly well, and is a great way of using up a glut of free hedgerow fruit. But it lacks the zingy 'lift' – the natural acidity – of blackcurrant cordial, and is more appealing when a sharper note is added, usually in the form of citrus juice (see tip below). I make this with ripe, juicy blackberries, heated in a pan with one third as much volume of water. Add sugar (a little at a time and keep tasting, to avoid oversugaring this already sweet fruit). Simmer slowly until reduced by one-third, then cool, strain, and bottle. It will keep for up to a month in the refrigerator.

* *Dilute according to taste, adding a splash of orange or other citrus juice to add the necessary tang.*

* *I use this as the base for a non-alcoholic, warm Hallowe'en brew, with cloves, cinnamon and slices of fruit added, eye of newt optional … kids love it.*

# Blackberry Wine

*Makes 4.5 litres
(8 pints)*

*Drink up within
6 months*

This country wine uses up a lot of brambles – great when it's an abundant crop and the wild bushes and hedgerows are heavy with fruit. It makes a pale red wine, almost in the style of a simple Beaujolais, Italian Bardolino or Australian Tarrango. Using this recipe, the result is off-dry, fruity and fresh. Serve very slightly chilled and drink as a refreshing aperitif or with savoury snacks.

**2.7kg (6lb) blackberries**
**4.5 litres (8 pints) boiling water**
**900g (2lb) sugar**
**2 lemons**
**½ tbsp citric acid**
**yeast and nutrient, according to the packet (see page 29)**

1. Pick over the blackberries and pull off any stubborn stalks, then wash in cold water and shake until semi-dry in a colander, batch by batch.
2. Put all the berries in a large preserving pan or clean bucket and pour the boiling water over them. Bring to a gentle simmer for 10 minutes. Turn the heat off.
3. Add the sugar and stir until dissolved, then the juice and pared rind of the lemons and the citric acid. Cover and leave overnight to steep and gradually cool down.
4. Strain through muslin into a sterile container, and add the yeast and nutrient. Stir well.
5. Pour into a demi-john, fixing an airlock and bung. Blackberry wine throws a lot of sediment so you may need to rack it off more than once after the fermentation has finished before bottling (see page 30).

* *This wine starts off a deep, inky, purple-red but lightens quite a lot during the fermentation – even if it is kept in the dark. After a month's ferment, expect a pale, ruby-red hue. The texture is light.*

* *The length and vigour of the fermentation will depend a great deal on the temperature of the room where you keep the wine (see also page 30) – September can be warm or cool, so bear that in mind.*

* *A good wine to sip lightly chilled with charcuterie: a plate of salami, chorizo and ham with a few tomatoes on the side is just perfect.*

# Crème de Mure (Blackberry Liqueur)

*Makes approximately
2½ litres (4½ pints)*

*Drink within
6 weeks*

What a discovery: a gorgeous, seductive, sensationally sweet liqueur that's rich, deep-purple and wonderfully warming. A shot of homemade crème de mure makes a great autumnal digestif, but you can do so many other things with it – mix it into cocktails, turn it into a long drink, use it in cooking …

The blackberries come free for many of us and so this is a clever alternative to crème de cassis if you don't grow (or want to buy) blackcurrants. But don't think of this liqueur as the 'poor cousin' to cassis, as it has a wonderful flavour all of its own. In fact, I know many people who prefer this blackberry version.

Now the downside: blackberry juice (and even more so, the red-wine-soused blackberry liqueur) stains terribly, so watch out. Mash the fruit up in a really big pan or bucket that can easily take the load, or be sure to wear black!

**1½kg (3lb 5oz) ripe blackberries
2 litres (3½ pints) red wine
1kg (2lb 4oz) sugar, possibly more to taste
70cl brandy or vodka (unflavoured)**

1. Pick over the blackberries, carefully removing the stalks and bits of leaf or twig. Discard any very bruised or rotten berries. Wash the lot, strain and then place in a very large preserving pan or clean bucket.
2. Crush the fruit well with a potato masher or put an electric hand blender over it all. Pour on the red wine and stir well. Cover and leave to steep for 48 hours, stirring from time to time.
3. Strain through a muslin bag into a sterilized container, squeezing the bag to get most of the liquid out (you might want to wear plastic gloves for this).
4. Rinse the original pan and pour the juice back in, now adding the sugar. Stir well. Heat up gently, still stirring, until the sugar has dissolved and the liquid is very hot, not boiling. Leave to reduce just under simmering point until the liquid thickens and turns slightly syrupy. This may take an hour or more. Stir occasionally.
5. Taste, and add more sugar if you think it needs it for flavour and texture. Leave to cool.
6. Add the spirit, stir well and pour into sterilized bottles.

* *Use a good-quality, freshly opened red wine to make this liqueur – nasty cheap red won't do! A fruity, medium-bodied style is spot on.*
* *Which spirit to use? Vodka is cheapest and works fine, but for a 'deluxe' version, use premium French brandy for its richer, fruity notes. Armagnac is especially good.*
* *Drink this up fairly quickly after making as it doesn't store as well as crème de cassis, losing its fresh aroma and fruity edge, perhaps because of its relatively low acidity.*
* *Crème de mure is very, very good with duck – reduce your liqueur further to make it thicker and more syrupy and serve with rare duck breast.*
* *It's also great for pouring over ice cream, chocolate cakes and tarts – even vanilla cheesecake.*

# Blackberry Whisky

*Makes 1 litre
(1¾ pints)*

*Will keep for a year
and possibly longer,
after the blackberries
are removed*

This is for the grown-ups on Hallowe'en, indeed all through the chillier months – and especially when there may be a head cold lurking. It's a cockle-warming, fruity, sweet and slightly spicy shot, the fruit taking away the more fiery, peppery edge of the whisky.

I've tried various spirit bases for a blackberry infusion, and they all work fine, and aren't hugely distinctive, so feel free to use vodka or gin as you prefer. But the wood-spice of Scotch whisky seems particularly well suited to brambles, and, for that matter, to the sometimes dreary period between October and Christmas.

**600g (1lb 5oz) ripe blackberries**
**300g (10½oz) sugar**
**1 litre (1¾ pints) Scotch whisky**

1. Pick over the blackberries, removing any stalks and leaves. Wash carefully, strain and dab with kitchen paper until dry.
2. Pack the fruit into a large, sterilized kilner jar (or two smaller ones) filling it about two-thirds full. Add all the sugar, then top up to the brim with whisky. Seal the jar and turn several times to mix.
3. Turn regularly during the next 24 hours until the sugar has dissolved.
4. This will be ready to drink after 3 weeks, although it is better if kept longer. Remove the blackberries after 6 weeks if not finished up, though, to ensure no rotten or woody flavours start to pervade.

＊ *Don't use a very smoky, peaty Islay whisky for this – it tastes too strong for the blackberries, and anyway, it would be a shame to waste it on an infusion! Go for a decent, reasonably priced blended Scotch.*

＊ *Serve at room temperature, as this winter warmer does not suit a chill.*

＊ *Try adding a splash to fruit compotes or red-berry pies and crumbles, for grown-ups only.*

# Elderberry Wine

*Makes 4.5 litres
(8 pints)*

*Enjoy within
2–6 months, as
this is when it
tastes most lively
and vibrantly fruity*

Elderflower drinks are tempting of course (see pages 42–45), but do, do leave enough blossom on the bushes to ensure you get a decent crop of elderberries, too, in September. They make one of our very best 'country wines', and it's a free hedgerow fruit, of course, which has very little other use, so once you see them getting ripe, pick 'em quick and start fermenting.

This is remarkably similar to a light, fresh, young red made from grapes – an Italian wine such as Bardolino or a young, simple Merlot. It's also aromatic, full of forest fruits, currrants and berries (and not just elderberries).

Go for the long-soak method to get as much extract, colour and fresh, fruity character as possible. The wine is on the medium-dry side rather than bone-dry; simply reduce the amount of sugar used if you prefer a more tart finish.

**1.5kg (3lb 5oz) elderberries**
**4½ litres (8 pints) boiling water**
**yeast and nutrient, according to the packet (see page 29)**
**1 tsp citric acid (see page 29)**
**1.3kg (3lb) brewer's sugar (see page 29)**

1. Strip the little purple berries off their stalks by using a small table fork and dragging down the bunches. The berries should pop right off in 1 or 2 drags: a really quick and strangely satisfying process. Make sure that you end up with 1.5kg (3lb 5oz) of berries.
2. Place the fruit in a preserving pan and crush evenly and thoroughly with a potato masher. Pour on the boiling water, stir, cover, and leave to cool.
3. Once the liquid has cooled to under 30°C (86°F), add the yeast and acid. Leave for 3 days, well covered with a permeable cloth, and stir from time to time.
4. Place the sugar in a sterilized container. Strain the cool elderberry juice through a muslin directly on to the sugar. Stir until the sugar has dissolved, then pour into a sterilized demi-john and fix an airlock and bung. Keep in a warm, dark spot. Fermentation can be long and slow in this case, but after it has finally finished, rack off and bottle (see page 34), preferably in dark glass bottles to retain the colour of the wine.

✶ *Serve at room temperature, or very slightly chilled if you want to enhance the succulent tang.*
✶ *A good Elderberry Wine is so much like a lightish, young red wine made from grapes that you can apply exactly the same serving ideas to it, so match it with:*
  * *simple meat dishes like ham salads and other cold meats, sausage rolls and charcuterie*
  * *mild cheeses, roast root vegetables or mushroom dishes, especially risotto*
  * *simple tomato- or meat-based pasta sauces.*

# Rosehip Syrup

Makes
approximately
2 litres (3½ pints)

Drink within
2 weeks

Sometimes it seems rosehips are everywhere in the late autumn and winter – in the garden, the woods, up the walls of the house and, of course, poking prettily out of the hedgerows. You can always use them for rosehip jelly, but I bet a cordial of hips, glowing orange and smelling surprisingly fruity, gets used up by the whole family more quickly and enthusiastically.

Rosehip syrup is said to contain more vitamin C than citrus fruit – another great reason to make the most of this free autumnal crop. This is a drink that was made extensively during rationing after World War II, but don't think of it as a 'make do and mend' type cordial; it is quite delicious. And kids adore it.

**900g (2lbs) rosehips**
**2.6 litres (4½ pints) boiling water**
**900ml (1½ pints) hot water**
**500g (1lb) sugar**

1. Top and tail the rosehips, and give them a good wash. No need to dry them, though.
2. Mince the damp fruits thoroughly in a food processor or blender. You might need to add a little cold water to mince them thoroughly, as they are quite sticky and bits can get caught in the blades.
3. Pour the 2.6 litres (4½ pints) of boiling water into a pan, tip in the minced fruit, bring back to the boil again and cook for a minute or two. Turn the heat off and leave for 15 minutes.
4. Strain through a muslin bag and retain the liquid, putting the pulp back into the pan. Add the 900ml (1½ pints) of hot water to the pulp, and bring to the boil again.
5. Turn the heat off and leave for 10 minutes this time.
6. Strain again, collecting both batches of hot liquid together, and discarding the pulp. Heat the liquid to simmering point, and cook till reduced by one-third.
7. Add the sugar, stir to dissolve and simmer gently for a further 5 minutes.
8. Allow to cool, pour into sterilized bottles and seal. Dilute to taste – most children will vote for it being strong and sweet!

* *Rosehip syrup doesn't keep particularly well. It soon loses its fruity, fresh aroma and general appeal, and after several weeks, may even ferment. Drink up within two weeks, then make some more.*
* *This is naturally cloudy, and an attractive peachy-orange colour.*
* *Sip it as a hot drink to ward off colds, adding a small piece of fresh, peeled root ginger to your cup..*
* *Mix it with a little ginger liqueur for grown-ups.*
* *Pour over pancakes or waffles for breakfast. Rosehip syrup is also delectable reduced down further and poured over creamy vanilla pannacotta, or spoon it over classic English rice puddings for a real taste of the 1950s.*

# Nettle Beer

*Makes 4.5 litres
(8 pints)*

*Takes time to mature
and mellow. Best
after 8 months'
ageing in bottle*

Shall I wax lyrical about the joys of picking nettles? No, it's a fairly unpleasant job – even though a vengeful joy can be found in doing something useful with such a pernicious and painful weed. Once you've got your nettles back home, process them quickly. The scent of cooking nettles is not terribly attractive (think earthy sprouts and spinach), but what I do find satisfying is turning the crop into an attractive, clear, sparkling beer. Eventually. Well, what else can you do with nettles, except a rather worthy soup? This is more fun.

**900g (2lb) young nettle tops**
**4½ litres (8 pints) boiling water**
**450g (1lb) sugar**
**14g (½oz) tartaric acid**
**2 lemons**
**5g brewer's yeast (see page 29)**
**1 tsp citric acid (see page 29)**

1. Wash the nettles and strain/shake off most of the water. Place in a large pan and pour on the boiling water. Bring back to a simmer and cook for 15 minutes.
2. Pour the sugar and tartaric acid into another large pan. When the nettle mix has cooled down a little, strain it directly on to the sugar and acid. Stir to dissolve.
3. Add the pared zest and juice of the lemons. Allow to cool, loosely covered for several hours.
4. Once under 30°C (86°F), add the yeast and citric acid and stir.
5. Strain again, pour into a sterilized demi-john and fit an airlock.
6. Once the fermentation has settled right down and nearly finished, which may take several weeks, rack the beer off into another sterilized demi-john, leaving behind the sediment.
7. Add a couple of teaspoons of caster sugar to prime the beer, stir and syphon into flip-top bottles (see opposite and page 27). Handle with care, as the second fermentation should give bubbles to the beer.
8. Store in a cool, shady place and leave for 8–12 months to mature.

* This recipe produces, in time, a nettle beer which tastes pleasantly grassy, off-dry and with a fruity, somewhat appley note.
* The second fermentation sometimes fails to 'take off' – if so, add a tiny bit more sugar and a minute pinch of yeast to the bottle and reseal. Beware exploding bottles, always looking away when opening.
* Nettle beer is a welcome and thirst-quenching draught with a ploughman's lunch of cheese, bread and salad (hold the pickles, which kill the delicate taste of the beer). Indeed, it goes best with anything bready/yeasty, such as savoury rolls, sandwiches, or crusty pizzas.

# Oak Leaf Wine

*Makes 4.5 litres (8 pints)*

*Drink after 6 months although this keeps for up to 2–3 years*

Oak Leaf Wine is well worth a try, but it seems to vary in character from batch to batch. The main reason is the time of year when you pick the leaves – young, bright-green leaves give a fresher, lighter wine, while late summer leaves deliver a richer, more tannic, nuttier style. Either way, this is not a wine to make in a hurry. Leave to ferment very slowly. It may bubble quietly for several months so simply leave it alone, and once fermented, keep in the demi-john. Certainly for a good year or so, it will only improve, becoming more mellow and complex. The colour is a beautiful, pale gold, the aroma slightly grassy with an interesting note of spiced orange, and the flavour is rich, viscous, with a citrus oil depth and a sweet but well-balanced finish. There's a (nice) note of sherry in there, and I can taste fresh wood, almost as though it has been aged in casks. The oaked quality strengthens with age – think traditional white Rioja. Fascinating, and it seems almost magical that wine can be produced from the juice and tannins of a bunch of leaves, but it can.

**4 litres (7 pints) oak leaves when pressed down lightly in a measuring jug**
**1kg (2lb 4oz) sugar**
**4½ litres (8 pints) boiling water**
**10g (¼oz) citric acid (see page 29)**
**yeast and nutrient, according to the packet (see page 29)**

1. Wash the leaves carefully, and pick over them, removing woody stalks and insects lurking on the backs or in folds. Chuck out bad leaves and shake the rest semi-dry.
2. Put the sugar into a large preserving pan or clean bucket and pour over the boiling water, stirring until the sugar has dissolved.
3. Bring the liquid back to the boil and when simmering, throw in all the oak leaves, pressing them down until they are covered. Stir well, and turn off the heat. Cover loosely and allow to infuse. Cool overnight.
4. A day later, squash the leaves down well using the back of large metal spoon, to extract a little extra character. Strain into a demi-john. Add the citric acid, yeast and nutrient and a little cold water to top up, if needed.
5. Fix the air-lock and bung and allow to ferment until clear, racking off at least once before bottling (see page 30).

* This is a strong, sweet, fairly weighty wine – and is quite different from those made with a fruit base.
* It's an interesting experiment to make two demi-johns and try them at different stages over a long period.

# Sloe Gin

*Makes 70cl*

*At its best after
1 year*

The extraordinary, bittersweet, almond and juniper flavour of sloe gin is rather unique – a classic winter drink. If you're lucky you'll know where to find sloes each autumn, but if the hard, dusty-matt, purple-blue berries prove elusive, look out for the white flowers of the blackthorn in spring. Come late autumn, that's your sloe bush!

Tradition dictates to wait until after the first hard frost of the autumn to pick sloes to get the best flavour, but you can treat an early crop to an icy blast in the freezer instead. Put the berries in overnight, then take them out and bruise them as they defrost by bashing with the back of a metal spoon. If you haven't frozen them, prick each individual berry with a needle to split the tough skin and release some juice (a rather fun job, I find, and so do my children). The most important thing is to get sloe gin made at least six weeks before Christmas, so it will be ready, albeit in a youthful, exuberantly fruity style, for the festive season. Older sloe gin tastes more rounded, mellow and even a little spicy.

**450g (1lb) sloes**
**450g (1lb) sugar**
**70cl gin**

1. Go through your crop, taking out any bruised, broken or marked sloes.
2. Freeze or prick the berries, as described above. Put them into a couple of medium-sized, sterilized flip-top bottles or kilner jars, sharing them out equally, and then pour equal amounts of sugar over them, adding up to 450g (1lb) in total.
3. Fill the bottles with gin and seal. Shake gently to kick-start the sugar dissolving.
4. Turn the bottles every hour or so for the first day, then once a day for the first week, then do it whenever the fancy takes you.
5. A wonderful pinkish-purple colour will start to seep out of the sloes after a few days.
6. Leave for at least 6 weeks, and preferably 10, before drinking (around Christmas). Sloe gin improves further with age, so keep one bottle for next year, although remove the sloes after 3 months and discard.

* *Add a few drops of almond essence to the gin when you first make it, if you want to emphasize the nutty, kernel-like quality of the drink.*

* *You don't have to discard the sloes after extracting. 'Slider' is made by adding the gin-soused sloes to good farmhouse cider, and leaving for 6-8 weeks until the liquid tastes of apples and sloes, with a hint of nut. A fun tradition from rural Devon.*

* *Top up with sparkling water and a dash of lime juice for a longer, more refreshing drink in warmer weather. Or try a Sloe Gin Fizz: mix equal shots of plain gin, Sloe Gin and lime juice, add a dash of sugar syrup and shake over ice. Strain into a tall tumbler and top up with cool soda water.*

* *A judicious splash of sloe gin gives an extra kick to autumnal fruit compotes, especially spiced red plums, or a blackberry-based mix.*

# Damson Gin

*Makes 70cl*

*Best enjoyed at
6–10 weeks, but
will keep longer.*

Just the same as the sloe recipe, but damsons give a sweeter, more juicy, plum-like liqueur; not gloopy, but rich, with a fine and appealing balance of sweet and sour in the fruit, and without the bitter character of sloes. Also, the actual 'gin' flavour is less obvious in the damson liqueur. Personally, I prefer damson; it's exquisite, although the fruit is much rarer than sloes (and more jealously guarded!). I make this in September and you certainly don't need to wait for a frost as you do with sloes, because damsons don't have such tough skins.

**450g (1lb) wild damsons**
**225g (8oz) sugar**
**70cl gin**

1. The damsons shouldn't need washing, but sort through and remove any bruised or rotten ones. Prick each damson 2 or 3 times with a needle.
2. Tip the fruit into a clean, sterilized jar (or jars) – note that you'll have trouble stuffing them into a very narrow-necked bottle. Pour in the sugar and top up with the gin.
3. Seal and shake to encourage the sugar to start dissolving, then turn gently every few days for between 8 and 12 weeks before drinking. If you are going to keep it for more than 3 months, strain off the damsons.

\* *Sweet and juicy, this is a delectable winter digestif.*

\* *Try serving a small shot with full-flavoured hard cheeses such as tangy farmhouse Cheddar.*

\* *Splash some into a rich gravy for game meats, especially pheasant or venison.*

\* *Don't discard the used damsons: remove the stones, chop, and stew them with sugar for use in sweet pies, or spoon over ice cream, or add them to a fresh lot for an extra kick to jam or jelly. Most of the alcohol in the gin-soaked fruit will cook off, but some gin-like flavour will linger.*

\* *The fruit below are bullace, thornless fruit that are sharp in taste but not bitter like sloes. If you happen to find these while foraging, try using them in place of sloes or damsons and make bullace gin.*

# Quince Vodka

*Makes*
*approximately*
*600ml (1 pint)*

I challenge anyone not to like this – quinces give the vodka a yellow glow and a honeyed flavour. This is another drink that you make in the autumn to be ready by Christmas. Another great gift, then.

**2 large quinces**
**50cl (18fl oz) vodka (unflavoured)**
**200g (7oz) golden caster sugar**

1. Wash and dry the quinces, then grate them, whole and unpeeled, using the coarse side of a grater. Use the entire fruit, core and all. As you grate, put batches into a kilner jar and splash in a little vodka, or the fruit will quickly brown.
2. Work swiftly and pile all the last bits into the jar and add the sugar, topping the whole lot up with the vodka.
3. Seal and turn gently to mix. Turn every day for 2 weeks, then occasionally for another 4 weeks. Strain after this period, discard the quince and bottle the lovely golden spirit.

＊ *This tastes quite sweet and doesn't need any more sugar adding at the end (as some recipes suggest).*

＊ *Delicious with a fresh fruit salad, or with a plate of preserved fruits (apricots, figs, dates), toasted hazelnuts and pistachios.*

＊ *I have made this with decent windfalls, but do inspect each quince carefully and discard any that are very bruised.*

# CITRUS DRINKS

Why bother making your own drinks out of citrus fruit when there are so many to choose from on the shop shelves? And when you are bound to be buying the fruit in, since you're hardly likely to grow large crops of oranges or lemons yourself? The answer is simple – because these citrus cordials are so good. They taste natural, juicy and exuberantly tangy, just as the fresh, ripe fruits do. How many shop-bought products can you say that about?

Make sure you buy unwaxed fruit wherever possible and try to choose organic. It is important to give the citrus fruit a good feel and ensure it is plump and ripe. If not, bring it home and ripen it on a warm windowsill, or, at a squeeze (sorry!), put it in the microwave for 30 seconds to bring out all those natural fruit juices. You don't need a fancy juicer or even a basic squeezer for these recipes; just stick a fork into one-half of any citrus fruit and twist the prongs round and round, pressing the skin as you go and collecting the juice in a large bowl.

Note: citric acid adds an extra tangy bite and acts as a preservative. I like it with lemon cordials, but not so much with the riper, more exotic flavours of mandarin and lime. But you can use it as you prefer.

# Lemon Cordial

*Makes (850ml)*
*1 ½ pints*

*Keeps for up to*
*2 weeks in the*
*refrigerator, or*
*freeze it in small*
*plastic bottles*

There are myriad recipes around for lemon cordial, but this is the best and it's fabulous – just the right balance between sweet and sour. It's my mum's recipe, and I've been drinking this for decades. It's just the thing to get anyone started making citrus cordials.

**1 lemon**
**300g (10½oz) sugar**
**850ml (1½ pints) boiling water**
**2 tsp citric acid (see page 29)**

1. Peel the lemon zest thinly, making sure you leave behind the white pith. Cut the pared lemon in half.
2. Put the zest in a large glass or plastic jug and squeeze the juice from the peeled lemon halves over the top. Make sure the water is at boiling point.
3. Pour the sugar over the fruit and then tip all the boiling water in, and stir well until the sugar is dissolved.
4. Add the citric acid and stir well again. Cover and leave overnight to cool and steep.
5. Strain through a sieve and bottle. Dilute to taste.

∗ *To make lemonade, dilute to taste with chilled sparkling water or soda.*

∗ *Try this recipe with 2 or 3 limes to 1 lemon and a little less sugar and citric acid – it's almost as good.*

∗ *Make up the concentrate in a glass jug with interesting additions such as bruised mint leaves (in summer), or ginger syrup from a jar of stem ginger (in winter).*

∗ *Add ice cubes, mint sprigs, slices of lemon and serve to party guests who don't want to drink alcohol – certainly beats fiercely fizzy shop-bought lemonade.*

∗ *Try serving this ice-cold with a shot of good vodka or gin – amazingly refreshing!*

# Pink Lemonade

Use the Lemon Cordial recipe, and throw in a handful of ripe fresh raspberries when you add the sugar and boiling water – these give a pink glow to the cordial and add a lovely juicy, red-berry dimension. Top up with chilled sparkling water or soda.

# Lemon Barley

Use the Lemon Cordial recipe, but when the cordial is ready to leave overnight, simmer 115g (4oz) pearl barley for 5 minutes, drain, rinse thoroughly and add to the mix to steep before straining. This gives a more complex, rather fuller, slightly malty quality.

# Mandarin and Lime Cordial

*Makes 300ml*
*(½ pint)*

*Keeps for up to*
*2 weeks in the*
*refrigerator, or*
*freeze it in small*
*plastic bottles*

Tried and tested, this aromatic, vivacious mix is the most popular (after pure lemon) of all the citrus cordial blends I make for my children and adult friends. Try it only when there are very big, juicy, ripe mandarins in the shops; it won't work well at all with drier, tougher fruit.

**6 large mandarin oranges**
**2 ripe limes**
**300ml (½ pint) water**
**100g (3½oz) sugar**

1. Halve and squeeze the fruit by hand (pips, zest and all) into a jug, then strain through a sieve into a medium-sized pan and pour over the water.
2. Bring to a gentle simmer and keep there, stirring occasionally, until reduced by one-third.
3. Turn off the heat and add the sugar, stirring until dissolved. Allow to cool.
4. Spoon off any pithy froth on the top and keep in the fridge. Dilute to taste.

✳ *Freeze this in ice-cube trays, popping out a small amount at a time to add to long drinks.*

✳ *Mix with cachaça or white rum and mint for an instant mojito with a burst of citrus flavour.*

✳ *Try this cordial with vegetarian stir-fries, mildly spiced prawns, or dishes flavoured with coriander.*

# St Clements

*Makes 300ml*
*(½ pint)*

*Keeps for up to*
*2 weeks in the*
*refrigerator, or*
*freeze it in small*
*plastic bottles*

A classic duo of orange and lemon with a little grapefruit thrown in for good measure – truly refreshing.

**4 large juicy oranges**
**1 lemon**
**1 grapefruit**
**300ml (½ pint) water**
**1 tsp citric acid (see page 29)**
**125g (4oz) sugar**

1. Halve each piece of fruit and squeeze them all into a jug. Pass the juice through a sieve into a large pan.
2. Pour the water over the fruit juices and bring to a gentle simmer.
3. Add the sugar and citric acid and stir over a low heat until dissolved. Simmer until reduced by one-third. Allow to cool.
4. Store in the fridge. Dilute to taste.

✳ *Diluted, this cordial on its own makes a refreshing breakfast drink (especially if you have run out of fresh juice), with flaky pastries and fresh fruit salad.*

✳ *Try this instead of orange juice for a twist on classic cocktails such as a Tequila Sunrise (with tequila and grenadine syrup), or a Big Easy (with Southern Comfort, Cointreau and ginger ale).*

✳ *This makes a delicious, non-alcoholic partner for fresh seafood – from prawns to scallops to clams.*

# Pink Grapefruit and Pomegranate Cordial

*Makes 250ml*
*(9fl oz)*

*Keeps for up to*
*2 weeks in the*
*refrigerator, or*
*freeze it in small*
*plastic bottles*

This is a gorgeous, rosy-hued cordial when diluted with cool, sparkling water, it's perhaps even better topped up with an icy, dry fizz such as cava, cremant or even Champagne.

Pink grapefruit can be a shade sweeter than white, so go steady on the sugar, or add more citric acid for extra zing. The addition of fresh, healthy pomegranate juice really makes this special – these two fruits have a natural affinity.

**4 large, ripe, pink grapefruit**
**200ml (7fl oz) water**
**75g (3oz) sugar**
**2 tsp citric acid (see page 29)**
**2 pomegranates**

1. Halve the grapefruits and squeeze their juice into a large jug. Sieve the juice into a large pan.
2. Pour the water into the pan and bring to a gentle simmer.
3. Add the sugar and citric acid and stir over a low heat to dissolve. Simmer gently to reduce by at least one-third. Allow to cool.
4. Collect the juice from the two pomegranates by halving them, then pulling out all the seeds from the centre with a fork. Mash the seeds coarsely to release the juice.
5. Sieve and add the pomegranate juice to the grapefruit cordial. Stir well.
6. Store in the fridge, spooning off any froth that rises to the surface after the liquid cools. Dilute to taste.

*✳ The perfect 'brunch' drink – it is delicious with eggs, toast and jams, or with jellies and fresh fruit.*

*✳ This cordial is especially good when made with sparkling water or soda.*

*✳ For a more boozy version, add a splash of tequila and top up with cold sparkling wine.*

# Lime, Ginger and Lemongrass Cordial

*Makes 500ml*
*(18 fl oz)*

*Keeps for up to*
*2 weeks in the*
*refrigerator, or*
*freeze it in small*
*plastic bottles*

This is something different – a scented, rather exotic cordial inspired by some of the shop-bought ones that go so well with Eastern cuisines, especially Thai. Surprise, surprise, this homemade version tastes better.

**10 lemongrass stalks**
**2 large knobs of fresh root ginger (approximately 5 x 3cm/2 x 1¼in)**
**6 fresh, ripe limes**
**500ml (18fl oz) boiling water**
**110g (4oz) sugar**

1. Top and tail the lemongrass stalks and peel off their roughest outer layers. Slice them lengthways then chop finely. Bruise the chopped pieces a little with a potato masher in a large bowl.
2. Peel the ginger and grate it roughly. Add to the lemongrass.
3. Pare the rind thinly from the limes and place in a large saucepan. Add the lemongrass and ginger mix and pour over the boiling water, followed by the juice of the limes.
4. Stir, heat and simmer for a couple of minutes, then turn off the heat and add the sugar, stirring until it dissolves. Steep the hot mixture for 1 hour.
5. Strain through a muslin bag, squeezing the last drops of liquid out of the bag by hand to release as much flavour as possible.
6. Bottle and keep in the fridge. Dilute to taste.

∗ *If you prefer a sweeter version of this cordial, add a large tablespoon (or even two, according to taste) of the luscious syrup from a jar of stem ginger to the final, cooled mix before bottling*

∗ *Try this cordial with fragrant Thai chicken, seafood and vegetable dishes that have coriander, lemongrass and perhaps coconut milk in the recipe.*

# Limoncello

*Makes 1.8 litres*
*(3 pints)*

*Keeps for years*

How many drinks are this mouthwatering yet powerful, fresh-tasting yet long-lived? Or, indeed, packed with tangy acidity, yet syrupy and thick – and are sipped after dinner as a digestif? At least, that's how they drink limoncello in southern Italy, especially along the Amalfi coast and in Sicily. Much as I'd like to be there right now, raising a glass, you can conjure up the same intensely lemony liqueur at home very easily indeed.

**5 ripe lemons, plus 1 for decorating finished bottles**
**1 litre (1¾ pints) vodka (unflavoured)**
**750g (1lb 10oz) sugar**
**700ml (1¼ pints) boiling water**

1. Pare the rind thinly from the lemons, taking care to avoid the white pith.
   Divide the rind between 2 large, clean glass jars – 1 litre (1¾-pint) kilner jars are perfect.
2. Pour the vodka over the lemon rind in the two jars, seal them and turn to mix.
3. Leave for 1 week, shaking the jars gently from time to time.
4. Place the sugar in a large heatproof bowl and pour the boiling water over the top, and stir well to dissolve.
5. While the sugar syrup is still hot, add the vodka and lemon-rind mix. Stir, cover and leave for 1 week.
6. Strain and divide between the cleaned jars, and add a few fresh strips of rind from a new lemon to each jar to decorate. Seal and keep forever.

✳ *Classic limoncello is made with Sorrento lemons, but any good-quality, unwaxed and preferably organic lemons will do.*

✳ *If drinking this as an after-dinner digestif, serve in shot glasses – chilling both glasses and limoncello well in advance.*

✳ *Dilute with sparkling water to make a gorgeous, zesty long drink, adding the juice of one fresh lemon per four drinks for extra zing.*

✳ *This is a great cocktail ingredient – use it to make Limoncello Martinis with equal parts vodka (unflavoured) and limoncello, and a small dash of fresh lemon juice, all shaken over ice and strained into chilled martini glasses.*

✳ *Pour over pancakes and/or ice cream, or use it to make a grown-up lemon drizzle cake. This makes a fabulous ingredient in lemon possets and syllabubs, too.*

# ORCHARD DRINKS

Every late autumn I stare in wonder at the beautiful crops of apples
and pears on the trees around where I live in southwest England.
And then I can hardly believe it when some of this fabulous fruit
is left to rot on the ground or to wither, even freeze, on the trees.
Sure, we have a great many apples in this particular corner of the
world, but someone must want to use this fruit?

Inexpensive supermarket apple juice is something we all take for
granted, but when you think about it, a lot of the cheaper stuff
made from concentrate doesn't actually taste that great. Press your
own and I bet you'll start freezing it in vast amounts. Cider is so simple
to make, so why not give that a go? And apple wine is a must for
anyone who has access to large amounts of orchard fruit. There's
a real community feel to the apple-picking and pressing season
round here, so try to find out who else is doing it round your way,
and get to the 'core' of these drinks …

# Pressing apples and pears for juice

It's a somewhat daunting, if enticing, sight: big baskets or sacks piled high with newly picked orchard fruit, some a little bruised, perhaps, some with leaves and twigs attached, even a pasting of mud and the odd insect crawling around the edge. Where on earth to start getting fresh, thirst-quenching juice out of that lot? Teamwork helps, and ganging up with others to crush works best – a press is expensive, so don't fork out for one before asking around (or even advertising locally) to find one you can borrow.

You'll no doubt be using whatever varieties you can get your hands on – a mongrel mixture of sweet dessert varieties, crisp, tart and, perhaps, cider apples or a small proportion of crab apples. The latter is best of all, so do muddle your batches of home-grown fruit together.

Have a close look at the fruit and only wash those that really need it. Muddy windfall apples and pears will certainly need an outdoor 'hose down'. Now the production line starts: work through the fruit, removing stalks and leaves, and cutting out and discarding any bruised, rotten or otherwise blemished bits (and give these to the pigs). Then chop the apples or pears into chunks (roughly, quartering any small fruit, and cutting larger ones into six or eight bits). Don't bother removing the core and certainly never peel them. Work fairly quickly or the cut fruit will oxidize badly. While one or two people chop, others pop the pieces into the crusher. The crushed fruit (called 'pomace') must be pressed swiftly and the precious liquid caught in clean buckets.

The results can look less than perfect – amber-brown, dense and cloudy – but homemade juice always seems to taste just wonderful. Bursting with fresh flavour, with a slightly tannic, dry finish and incisive, crisp, mouthwatering acidity. You may decide to dilute the juice with water a little at this point. Either way, freeze any that you won't be drinking as juice, or fermenting into cider, as quickly as possible – I use old but sterilized plastic milk and juice cartons for this, leaving a little space for the liquid to expand on freezing. Ensure the crusher is cleaned thoroughly. Ferment the liquid sooner rather than later to preserve as much freshness in the raw ingredient you are using – your own, hand-pressed orchard juice.

PS: I know some who use shop-bought apple and pear juice to make cider and perry. If you must, give this a go using the best, cloudy, fresh juice you can buy and follow the same recipes in this chapter, but it won't be a patch on the home-pressed stuff, and you won't have as much fun getting it!

# Apple Cider

*Makes 4.5 litres*
*(8 pints)*

*Keeps up to*
*12 months*

For the serious cider maker there are plenty of books that will take you down the 'advanced' route, suggesting particular apple varieties, or blends of varieties, commenting on yeast strains, etc. But for the rest of us, cider couldn't be easier – it is simple, fermented apple juice.

One important tip: take your newly pressed apple juice, taste it, and if you really think it needs sugar, add it. But most juices that have been made from a balanced mix of ripe, sweet and acidic/bitter apples don't require more sweetening (and note that adding sugar could make your cider much stronger). I use the same type of yeast as for fruit wines, but you can buy special cider yeast strains at home-brew shops if you prefer. Or why not make several demi-johns of cider using different yeast strains and see which works best for you?

**4.5 litres (8 pints) fresh apple juice, a mix of sweet, acid and bitter varieties**
**yeast and nutrient, according to packet (see page 29)**

1. Bring the apple juice to room temperature if it has been chilled.
2. Strain it through fine muslin or a sieve into a large, sterile container to remove any fine solids. Add the yeast.
3. Using a clean jug and a funnel, carefully pour it into a sterilized demi-john and fix an airlock and bung.
4. Treat just as you would a fruit wine, waiting until the fermentation has finished (or very nearly finished) before racking off once or twice (see page 30) and either maturing in the demi-john or bottling.

✳ *Cider fermentations seem to be very vigorous at first, so you might want to rest the demi-john in a plastic bucket or tray in case the froth spills over. Clean the airlock and bung after such an occurrence, or you could opt to use a small glass, placed upside down over the demi-john neck, instead of an airlock and bung at first, though fit the latter after things calm down a little.*

✳ *Homemade cider tastes much, much better if left to ferment slowly through many weeks and then matured in the demi-john or bottle for several more months.*

✳ *Your cider should be flat, not fizzy, as all traditional ciders are. If you want to make a sparkling version, see the method for Perry on page 100.*

✳ *You will have to use a hydrometer both before and after fermentation to work out the strength of your cider (see page 27), but if you don't, always assume it is on the strong side – it certainly isn't likely to be weak!*

✳ *Enjoy lightly chilled homemade cider with the classic English 'ploughman's' plate of Cheddar cheese, crusty bread and mild pickles. It also goes well with roast pork and apple sauce, premium sausages, cold chicken and cheese-topped vegetable bakes.*

# Apple Wine

Don't miss out on making apple wine because of the universal appeal of the freshly pressed juice and cider. It is quite delicious, and a great way of using up an orchard glut. Choose notably ripe fruit – using windfalls is also fine as long as you cut away any rotten or bruised pieces. I'm sure you will use whichever varieties are growing nearby, but some are better than others – my neighbour makes a terrific version from the Beauty of Bath variety, for example. This recipe makes a fairly dry style; and note the major difference between the method for Apple Wine and Cider – for this wine recipe, the apples are cooked first.

**3.5kg (7lb 13oz) apples**
**4.5 litres (8 pints) water**
**1.2kg (2lb 11oz) sugar**
**1 tsp citric acid (see page 29)**
**yeast and nutrient, according to the packet (see page 29)**

1. Wash the apples well, snip off any stray stalks and leaves and cut away any brown or blemished bits. Keep all healthy peel on the fruit.
2. Chop the fruit into small pieces.
3. Bring the water to the boil in a large preserving pan. Add the apple pieces, stir them in and simmer gently for 15 minutes. Let the liquid cool for a few minutes until warm rather than hot.
4. Place the sugar and citric acid in another large, clean container and strain the warm liquid through muslin on to it, stirring until it has all dissolved. Let the liquid cool.
5. When the liquid has cooled to under 30°C (86°F), add the yeast and nutrient, and, using a funnel, pour into a sterilized demi-john, fixing an airlock and bung.
6. When the fermentation is finished, rack off the wine (see page 30) and bottle it (see below).

\* *Try to get some more acidic apples into the mix here, even a small proportion of crab apples, to add tang and tannins to the flavour of ordinary eating apples.*

\* *Use a normal wine yeast here. Home-brew author CJJ Berry says a 'Sauternes' yeast is best of all; I use a Champagne yeast.*

\* *This Apple Wine definitely improves with age and should be left for at least six months once bottled in a cool, dark place before drinking.*

# Spiced Apple Cup

*Makes 3 litres
(about 5¼ pints)*

*Best enjoyed on
the day it is made*

Just the thing to keep spirits raised on a cold, windy autumn evening, or, indeed, Sunday lunch. I always make this after the troops have been pressing fruit in the yard as a 'thank you', and I give it to chilly grown-ups who are accompanying the 'trick and treaters' at Hallowe'en too. You can use apple juice for a 'soft' version or apple cider for an alcoholic version, adding a splash of apple brandy (not homemade, use English apple brandy or French Normandy's Calvados) for an even headier brew!

**3 litres (5¼ pints) fresh apple juice or still cider**
**3 whole cloves**
**3 cinnamon sticks**
**5cm (2in) knob of fresh root ginger, peeled and cut into thin slices**
**3 whole allspice berries**
**juice of half a lemon**
**a little runny honey or soft brown sugar (optional, quantity to your own taste)**
**apple brandy (optional for cider version only)**
**2 organic green and red eating apples (for garnish)**

1. Pour the cider or apple juice into a large pan and add all the spices.
2. Heat gently to just under simmering point, stirring from time to time with a long-handled ladle, and making sure the drink doesn't boil too hard. Taste from time to time as you go and if any spice seems especially strong, remove it and discard.
3. Add the honey or sugar, if using, little by little, tasting as you go. Then do the same with the lemon juice and brandy, if using, until just the right balance has been found.
4. Quarter, core, and slice (but don't peel) the apples and pop the slices in for the last minute or two before serving.
5. Ladle into thick glass tumblers, making sure every drink has a clove, or a bit of cinnamon and some apple slices. Serve immediately.

# Pear Juice, Pear Wine and Perry

If you substitute pears for apples in the recipes in this chapter, you can easily make pear wine and perry. Use fairly ripe pears – not sour, hard ones – where possible, and (in an ideal world) a good mix of tart and sweet varieties for a fine balance in the finished drink.

To make sparkling Perry, follow the recipe for Apple Cider, using pears instead, then bottle the finished liquid in strong flip-top bottles, adding a little sugar to 'prime' (see page 29), then store and wait for the yeast to create bubbles, which will be trapped inside the bottle.

Be careful when opening in case pressure has built up – point the bottle away from your face (and anyone else's) and slowly ease the top off. Perry usually has subtle, delicate flavours and as such makes a delightful aperitif, or serve it with light savoury snacks at a party, such as little savoury cheese pastries, for example.

Here's a refreshing, aromatic Pear and Elderflower Cocktail which can also be made as a refreshing long mocktail for non-drinkers or children, simply by dropping the vodka in favour of chilled soda water.
1. Use 2 parts plain vodka and 2 parts fresh pear juice, to 1 part homemade elderflower cordial concentrate, a splash of lime juice and a drop of sugar syrup (or runny honey).
2. Shake the vodka, pear juice and cordial in a classic cocktail shaker over ice.
3. Strain into tumblers over more ice, squeeze in the lime and sweeten to taste. For the soft version, leave out the vodka, shaking only the pear juice and cordial (or simply stir over ice in a jug), strain into tall glasses or cups with ice, and add the lime and sweet stuff.
4. Top up with plenty of soda.
5. Decorate both drinks with lime slices and mint leaves.

# OTHER WINES AND GRAPE DRINKS

Homemade wine made from grapes? Brilliant! Except that there are thousands of very cheap wines crowding our shop shelves, and, truly, many of them are just as palatable as anything you can make at home. I'd rather create my own wine and other drinks out of something different – preferably wild, free or glut produce – and buy my fermented grape juice from a good merchant or store. And if you buy a short-cut 'wine kit' containing grape concentrate, it should come with its own, perfectly clear instructions. Instead, I make fresh grape juice from time to time when people give me home-grown grapes, and even occasionally, from shop-bought ones – kids absolutely love it.

So, would-be serious oenophiles should look for a complete, in-depth manual to grape-growing and production. Here, instead, is my joyous take on grape juice, and two more recipes for country wines, which (usefully) can be made all year round, but tend to be my 'winter ferments'. This is because the key ingredients – parsnip, rice and raisins – can be sourced easily in the colder months.

# Parsnip Wine

*Makes approximately
4.5 litres (8 pints)*

*Keeps for 1 year*

There are countless recipes for making wine from vegetables, most of which aren't terribly tempting, but I'm glad I discovered parsnip wine. This sweet-tasting, cheap root vegetable (which you might have in the allotment) makes a good base ingredient for wine at exactly the moment when many other raw, glut ingredients are completely finished for the year. I make it in November and it is ready by mid-January. The colour of parsnip wine is an appealing creamy white; the flavour is medium-dry, rather honeyed, juicy and full-bodied. If you like off-dry, fruity Riesling or Pinot Gris, then this is for you.

This (apparently 'very old') wine is slightly adapted from *The Eynsham Cookbook*, a collection of recipes donated by villagers in my hometown, west of Oxford.

**2.25kg (5lb) parsnips**
**4.5 litres (8 pints) water**
**1.3kg (3lb) sugar**
**juice of 1 orange, strained**
**juice of 1 lemon, strained**
**yeast and nutrient, according to the packet (see page 29)**

1. Don't peel the parsnips, but give them a quick wash and then top and tail them, finally chopping them into medium-sized chunks and slices.
2. Put the parsnips in a large preserving pan and add the water. Bring to the boil.
3. Simmer for about 30 minutes or until the parsnip pieces are soft.
4. Let the pan cool a bit, until ready to handle, then strain through muslin or a fine sieve into a second large pan or clean bucket. Discard the parsnip pieces (pigs love 'em!).
5. Add the sugar to the warm liquid, followed by the citrus juices.
6. Bring to the boil and simmer for 20 minutes.
7. Cool, adding yeast and nutrient when under 30°C (86°F).
   Pour into a sterilized demi-john, top up with cold water if necessary and fix an airlock and bung.
8. After several weeks' fermentation (this will depend on how cold the weather is), rack off and bottle.

* *Parsnip wine should be clear, with none of the creamy-cloudiness of the fermenting liquid. However, fermentation is slow – partly because it is usually made in the colder winter months. Patience is needed.*

* *Try a glass of parsnip wine with cold pork and chicken, or cheesy quiches and savoury tarts, or a good cheeseboard and chunks of crusty bread.*

# Red Grape Juice

Very roughly, you
can expect around
150ml (¼pint)
from 450g (1lb)
of grapes

Best enjoyed on the
day it is made

Now, this definitely is well worth making on a small scale. My children absolutely adore it, and it's a wise alternative to wine for us, too, sometimes. It's something fun to do with the fruit of just one productive vine that you might have growing at home, either outside or (in cooler climates) in a greenhouse or conservatory. Here is the best method.

1. Make sure your grapes are ripe and taste sweet – keep trying one or two to assess! Cut off the bunches using sharp secateurs, collecting the fruit in small batches in a basket. Only pick the grapes close to the time you are going to make the juice, as the fruit will start to taste less fresh pretty quickly.
2. Remove the grapes from all the stalks – large and small – and discard any green, very hard, or old and mouldy berries. Wash the grapes well in cold water and shake dry over the sink.
3. Now put the grapes into a pan (a big preserving pan if processing in bulk) and mash them with a potato masher, just enough to crush each berry and remove most of the juice, but not so roughly that you reduce everything to a complete mush and risk getting too many dry-tasting tannins from the skins.
4. Add enough water to come up 5cm (2in) from the bottom of the pan, and simmer the grapes for 10 minutes, stirring from time to time to stop the skins sticking to the bottom. Taste a little of the red liquid and add some sugar to taste if required. Stir to dissolve.
5. Strain through a fine sieve or muslin and let cool. Dilute with cold sparkling water to taste.

* You can follow exactly the same process with white grapes, though the results are less interesting and white juice lacks some of the health benefits of red.

* For rosé juice, crush the red grapes only a little and run off the lightly stained liquid quickly before the colour turns properly red. The juice will taste fresh and fruity, but not as rich as red grape juice.

* Try mixing red grape juice with shop-bought cranberry or pomegranate juice for a ruddy, rich, healthy glassful bursting with antioxidants.

* Drink as soon as it is made in the case of pink or white, and red within two hours – grape juice doesn't keep well, and it doesn't freeze well, either.

# Rice and Raisin Wine

*Makes approximately
4.5 litres (8 pints)*

*Keeps for 6 months*

This is another wine that can be made all year round, so it's a useful recipe to have when any seasonal crops are finished. I make it in winter, so the colder temperatures and lack of summer flies mean I don't worry too much about this being an 'open' ferment. Indeed, this is the only wine in the book that I allow to ferment in an open container for a long time, but since it is not based on fresh fruit, I am not aiming for bright, zesty flavours anyway. It should be said that the results are can vary from batch to batch, probably because of the raisins. You should end up with a powerful, off-dry, amber-coloured wine with the flavour of raisin still very much present, but this is one that strangely fails from time to time. You could try boiling the raisins briefly after chopping and before using in the mix, if concerned, or adopt a laid-back attitude to this one … it hardly costs much to give it a try, and when it works, it is good.

**1kg (2lb 4oz) uncooked white rice**
**4.5 litres (8 pints) cold water**
**800g (1lb 12oz) sugar**
**800g (1lb 12oz) raisins**
**juice of 1 orange, or 2 juicy satsumas**
**juice of 1 lemon**
**yeast and nutrient, according to the packet (see page 29)**

1. Wash the rice well and leave in a sieve to drip until partially dry.
2. Pour half a litre of the water into a medium pan and bring to the boil. Add all the sugar and stir until completely dissolved. Let the solution cool to lukewarm.
3. Chop the raisins very roughly with a large serrated knife in small batches on a chopping board. This is to release some of the juices. Now put the raisins, rice and citrus juices into a sterilized preserving pan, or a large, sterilized bucket.
4. Heat the remaining water until hand-hot.
5. Pour the sugar solution on to the rice and raisin mix, followed by the rest of the water and stir well. Cover loosely (I use clean tea towels) and let it cool until under 30°C (86°F).
6. Add the yeast and nutrient and give it a stir. Cover loosely again and leave in a warm place for 7 days to ferment.
7. Strain the fermenting mix through muslin, discard the solids and pour the liquid into a demi-john, topping up with cold water if needed, and fixing an airlock and bung.
8. Once fermentation is over – and it should be relatively quick here – rack off (see page 30) and bottle.

# HONEY AND GINGER DRINKS

Honey oozes up to the surface now and again throughout this book, especially as a natural sweetener for hot toddies and teas. It's a most useful commodity, so great news when you find a source of honey nearby – especially as stocks are currently relatively scarce around the world. Do try to smoke out local bee-keepers who will sell you honey, or perhaps even trade you some for a finished drink. Otherwise, shop-bought honey is fine, but make sure you buy the clear, runny version, not the cloudy, solid stuff. And although the cheaper brands are perfectly okay, if you trade-up to top-quality honey, the results will taste better for it.

As for ginger drinks, you might have noticed how much fresh ginger is used in this book. Homemade ginger drinks are among my very favourites. Ginger is fabulous – I love the unique, sweetened, juicy heat of the fresh root, and its lovely aroma when heated.

Ginger – both fresh and ground – is cheap, easily sourced and wonderfully versatile. See other uses for this useful ingredient on pages 87, 121 and 134. I especially like the fact that there are lots of non-alcoholic or very low alcohol drinks made from ginger, as well as strong, heady ones, so you can tailor the drinks to suit children or drivers. Here are three drinks that press this humble, knobbly rhizome into service.

# Mead

*Makes 4.5 litres
(8 pints)*

*Keeps for several
years, but is best
drunk between
6–18 months after
fermentation*

To read some of the available information you'd think mead was more difficult to make than any other drink in this book. Yet, that hasn't been my experience. I find mead to be pretty easy stuff. This is a straightforward, no-nonsense recipe for medium-dry mead adapted from a recipe in CJJ Berry's indispensable *First Steps in Winemaking*. It works; enough said.

**1.5kg (3lb 5oz) English honey (or whatever is local to you)**
**4.5 litres (8 pints) cold water**
**1 orange**
**1 lemon**
**yeast and nutrient, according to the packet (see page 29)**

1. Pour the honey into a large pan, add the water and heat to just under simmering point Simmer for half an hour, stirring until the honey is dissolved. Skim off any froth, then pour into a clean container (a preserving pan or bucket) and let cool.
2. Once the liquid is quite cool, add the strained juice of the citrus fruits and an all-purpose wine yeast with nutrient.
3. Pour into a demi-john and fit an airlock and bung.
4. Wait until fermentation has finished – this may take longer than for fruit wines – about 2 months (depending on the weather; the colder it is, the longer it takes). Rack off and bottle.

✳ *Clover honey is said to be the very best of all for this, as it gives a gentle, slightly grassy or floral note.*

✳ *Be careful not to boil the honey/water mix too hard, otherwise it can lose its delicate aroma and flavour.*

✳ *You must use a wine yeast with nutrient here because honey doesn't provide enough 'food' for the yeast on its own.*

✳ *To make a sweeter mead, simply increase the quantity of honey used to 2kg (4lbs).*

✳ *Match medium-dry mead with mildly spicy food, a good cheeseboard and pork, ham and chicken. Rule of thumb: if a meat goes well with a honey sauce or marinade, then it will be great with a glass of mead.*

# Metheglin (Spiced Mead)

The gentle flavour of honey takes well to the addition of aromatic spices, just watch out that you don't overwhelm the honey with too many cloves, in particular.

Stick to the same basic recipe as above, but before step 1, add 2 teabags and a muslin bag containing 4 cloves, 2 sticks of cinnamon, 6 thin slices of fresh ginger root, 1 tbsp of caraway seeds and the pared and sliced rind of the orange to 4.5 litres (8 pints) of very hot water to steep before using.

Remove the teabags after 5 minutes and the muslin bag after 30 minutes. Reheat the water until very hot before pouring over the honey, then proceed to step 1 and follow the method as above.

* *Spiced Mead is quite irresistible made into a hot toddy, with a slice of apple, another clove and possibly a small splash of brandy or Calvados in each glass tumbler.*
* *Try it with mildly spiced food – sounds obvious, but with peppery Szechuan food, and stir-fries with a little chilli pepper, it makes a star match!*
* *It is worth noting the Welsh word for metheglin (which sounds like a chemical); it is meddeglyn, which is more appealing, somehow.*

# Fruity Ginger Ale (non-alcoholic)

*Makes 500ml (18fl oz) of concentrate*

*Keeps for a week or so in the refrigerator*

This is a great one to whip up in a short time when you're expecting guests (young and old) and the weather is warm. It's popular with grown-ups, and goes down much better than boring orange juice when you need a soft drink to offer to drivers or other non-drinkers at a summer dinner party. You will find the concentrate very strong, sweet and peppery, so add plenty of lime and soda water to taste, particularly for children.

**150g (5½oz) fresh ginger root**
**600ml (1 pint) water**
**185g (6¼oz) sugar**
**soda water, dilute to taste (buy a big bottle and keep it in the refrigerator)**
**fresh limes, at least ½ per drink**

1. Peel and then grate the ginger coarsely.
2. Heat 400ml (14fl oz) water in a medium-sized pan until it's boiling.
3. Add the ginger, reduce the heat and simmer gently for 5 minutes.
   Remove from the heat, cover and let the mixture steep for 30 minutes.
4. Strain through muslin or a fine-mesh sieve. Squeeze or press the ginger a little to remove more juice. Discard the ginger as most of the flavour will have gone.
5. Rinse the pan and add the rest of the water (200ml/7fl oz) and bring it to the boil. Add the sugar, stirring to dissolve. Let the syrup cool.
6. Mix the ginger water with the sugar syrup. Keep in the fridge and dilute to taste with cold soda water and a good squeeze of lime juice per glass. Add ice and a lime wedge to each drink.

* *For a sweeter, richer depth of flavour use demerara sugar instead of granulated.*
* *You can make a mildly spiced version by adding 3 allspice berries, 1 whole star anise and half a stick of cinnamon to the ginger and water mix at the start of step 3.*
* *Make sure to use the very freshest ginger root you can find for this. It should snap when you pull off a nobbly bit, not bend.*
* *This is, of course, a really refreshing drink, and it goes extremely well with spicy, savoury food. 'Instant' ginger beers like this are popular in West Africa and suit the African spicy stews, especially those based on root vegetables.*

# Ginger Beer

*Makes 2 litres*
*(3½ pints)*

*Keeps for 7 days in*
*the refrigerator*

Some swear by a ginger 'plant' – a concentrate made with sugar, ground ginger and yeast, which can be divided and used again and again – but I found that I rarely bothered with the rest of the plant after making just one batch of beer. This quick and easy recipe, using fresh ginger, does away with all the fiddle and makes a tasty ginger brew in two or three days. A word to the wise (and parents): this is, of course, mildly alcoholic. And please note all the cautions about exploding bottles.

**1½ tbsp fresh ginger root, peeled and grated**
**200g (7oz) sugar**
**½ tsp cream of tartar**
**1 lemon**
**½ tsp fast-action baker's yeast**
**2 litres (3½ pints) cold water**

1. Place the grated ginger, sugar, cream of tartar and 500ml (18fl oz) of the cold water in a large saucepan and bring to the boil.
2. Cut the lemon in half, squeeze the juice of both halves into the pan, then add in one half to boil, discarding the other – the lemon flavour is too strong with both.
3. Simmer for 5–10 minutes, stirring to dissolve the sugar.
4. Add the remaining 1.5 litres (2¾ pints) of the cold water and let the liquid cool until it reaches room temperature.
5. Sprinkle on the yeast, stir in and leave for several hours covered well with a clean tea towel.
6. Strain the liquid through a fine-mesh sieve, pressing down the ginger bits in the sieve to extract any last bit of flavour.
7. Using a funnel or thin-lipped jug, pour into 2 x 1-litre (1¾ pints) sterilized, plastic soft drinks bottles, leaving a little room at the top for the carbon dioxide to take up room. Make sure the last, yeasty-thick drops of the liquor are divided between the 2 bottles.
8. Seal and store in a cool, dark place for 2–3 days, loosening and resealing the tops from time to time to release the pressure of the gas. The Ginger Beer should be ready after 3 days.
9. Open with extreme caution at all times – the beer will be under pressure from the fermentation process, especially in hot weather. Never point the bottle in someone's face (including your own).

* *Never use glass bottles while the Ginger Beer is fermenting in case they shatter. Once fermentation has died right down (after several days), you can decant to a prettier flip-top bottle if you like, but continue to treat with caution.*

* *Use your Ginger Beer as a mixer with spirits and with elderflower cordial, or simply add some bruised mint leaves and loads of ice.*

* *Cold Ginger Beer is incredibly refreshing on a hot day, and washes down mildly spicy seafood, such as stir-fried prawns with chilli, ginger and coriander, brilliantly. Try it with savoury tarts and quiches, too.*

* *You can also make a hedonistic ginger liqueur by mixing grated fresh ginger with vodka. Leave the mixture to steep for 5–6 days, strain into bottles and then, for each 700ml (about 1 pint) of vodka, add a solution made from 250ml (8fl oz) of water and 125g (4oz) sugar, shake and serve. Delicious!*

# TEAS, TISANES AND SPICY BREWS

Boil water, pour it over a clutch of fresh leaves or a sprinkling of aromatic spices, wait a few minutes, then drink. Making your own hot teas (or tisanes, if you want to be posh) is about as easy as it gets. And the results are often far better than from shop-bought herbal teas. Actually, some of the latter are quite unpleasant in my view, and they will cost you. Why pay out for a sullen yellow brew that smells of an old compost heap? Far better to make your own fresh-tasting, aromatic version.

Some ingredients work much, much better than others. And certain teas have health benefits, so it is claimed. Here, then, is a collection of the quickest, cheapest, simplest and tastiest home brews, with tips on how to serve them. Put the kettle on …

# Mint Tea

Is mint tea the most refreshing drink in the world? Probably. It's versatile, too – a hot, minty brew really picks you up in cold weather, while frosty, iced mint tea is a thirst-slaker in the summer. The basic method hardly needs explaining – pour very hot water on to fresh mint leaves, natch (approximately 5 leaves per cup) – but below are some tips that you might not have considered.

* *Always wash the mint and pick it over, removing any remotely woody stalks. Try to use the tender tips and first few leaves only, smaller stalks attached. For a stronger flavour, bruise the leaves a little with a spoon when in the hot water.*
* *Try experimenting with different types of mint; it's easy to source household mint, but Moroccan mint (available in most good garden centres) has a slightly better flavour. Or use spearmint.*
* *Use any combination of different mints and call it 'Three Mint Tea' or 'Four …' when you serve it to your friends. Sounds complex, but it's very easy.*
* *Make Iced Mint Tea by starting with a hot brew, remove the mint leaves after a few minutes and then chill the tea. Chuck ice cubes into tumblers and pour in the cool tea, garnishing with fresh mint sprigs.*
* *Mint and lemon go well together so try bruising a fresh lemon wedge with the back of a teaspoon as well as some mint sprigs in a cup of very hot water.*
* *A blend of black or green tea with fresh mint leaves is delicious.*
* *Sweeten any mint tea with sugar to taste – white sugar has a better flavour with mint than other sweetening agents.*

# Lemon Verbena Tea

You'll need fresh leaves for Lemon Verbena Tea; the dried stuff just doesn't cut it. This is a seasonal drink, and one that's treasured for its lovely aroma. The flavour is more delicate than the scent, with a distinctive citrus, lemon-peel tang. Use approximately 3 leaves per cup – no more, or the aroma gets a bit much. Tear each leaf into three or four pieces and put in the cup or kettle, pouring on boiling water. Steep for a few minutes, then strain and serve. Most people prefer a dab of honey added. Lemon Verbena Tea is said to help cure indigestion, insomnia and bad nerves. I'll drink to that.

# Raspberry Leaf Tea

There's plenty of anecdotal evidence to suggest that drinking Raspberry Leaf Tea can help bring on labour, and once contractions are underway, help soothe pain – not much hard evidence for this, though. Whatever the case, the leaves of the raspberry plant (*Rubus idaeus*) are packed with vitamins and minerals, and in dried form they make a tasty, fruity tea. Please don't take it in earlier stages of pregnancy, just in case.

Pick the raspberry leaves and wash them. Leave to dry out completely in a warm place (in an airing cupboard or in reliable sunshine), then scrunch up into bits. Add a couple of teaspoons of the crushed leaves to each mug of freshly boiled water, steep for a few minutes, then strain. Add honey to taste.

* *Kids seem to like this, too – and it's good for slightly upset tums (anecdotal evidence, again).*

# Lemon Balm Tea

We have loads of lemon balm in the garden and often make tea from the fresh leaves. The delicate, citrus-based aroma and flavour are quite distinctive and make a gentle, soothing tea. Lemon Balm Tea is said to ward off just about everything from cold sores to menstrual cramps and insomnia to that scary catch-all 'old age'. Since the leaves come free and the flavour is very appealing, why not give it a go? I use approximately 8 leaves in a large teapot of freshly boiled water. You can serve this drink hot or iced, and do add a slice of lemon and a sprig of mint in warm weather (as lemon balm is a member of the mint family).

# Camomile Tea

Camomile tea is said to be a relaxant, and also good for the digestive system, which explains why so many people take a cup late at night, especially after a big meal. This is one of the most popular packaged teas you can find, but a homemade version is miles better than shop-bought dried camomile products. Brew up a teaspoon or two of crushed leaves from a fresh camomile plant and steep in very hot water for 10 minutes. Cover while it is brewing to stop volatile oils dissipating. A little honey can be added to taste. N.B. Those taking blood-thinning medication should not drink camomile tea.

# Fennel Tea

The slightly sweet, clean, aniseed flavour of tea made from crushed fennel seeds has real appeal. Use fennel seeds from plants you've grown in the garden for culinary use, or look out for commonly found wild fennel plants, or just use dried fennel seeds from a spice pot. Crush the seeds (one tablespoon per person) a little in a pestle and mortar, then put in a cup and pour over freshly boiled water. Steep for 5 minutes, strain and drink. This is said to help ease colic, wind, IBS and sore throats. Fennel is also believed to be an aphrodisiac (easing the wind undoubtedly helps here).

Try mixing fennel with ginger (a few slices of fresh or a teaspoon of ground) or even a slice or two of the southwest Asian root galangal, or both, in a hot brew for a really warming cup.

# Thyme and Sage Teas

The aromatic leaves of thyme make a tea that is especially good for colds, coughs and bronchial congestion. Use fresh or dried thyme, and cover the pot while it is steeping to retain the oils. Inhale the steam as you sip. Use lemon thyme, with a squeeze of lemon juice, for a freshly scented, tangier version.

Sage is the herb to go for if you have mouth ulcers or bad gums – I suggest sipping and gargling the brew. A more tasty blend is thyme and sage leaves (a few of each), with a lightly bruised rosemary sprig and 5 slices of fresh ginger to a normal-sized teapot. Steep for 8 minutes and pour.

# Citrus and Spice Tea

This blend comes, via my editor at *Stella* magazine, from the L'Epi Dupin restaurant in Paris. Take 1 slice each of fresh orange and lemon, 1 star anise, 1 sprig of fresh mint and approximately a third of a stick of cinnamon. Stir into freshly boiled hot water, wait a few minutes and sip – you can strain it if you prefer.

# Star Anise, Cinnamon and Ginger Tea

Place 1 star anise, 1 short 'nub' of cinnamon (approximately a third of a stick) and 2 slices of peeled, fresh ginger root in a cup, pour over boiling water and let steep. Strain and sweeten with honey or (nice, this) a teaspoon of the syrup from a jar of stem ginger.

# Homemade Chai (simple version)

I like to make a pot of very weak black tea (so a little caffeine, yes), adding 2 fresh bay leaves, 2 cloves and 3 lightly crushed cardamom pods. Strain and add honey or sugar to taste. Easy.

# Masala Chai

This tea is highly fragranced, sweet and not too spicy if you go steady on the cloves – many recipes suggest far too much of this pungent spice. One very indulgent alternative is to replace the milk and sugar with half a cup of hot chocolate at the end. Either way, this makes two large mugfuls. It's especially good when snowed in and fed up, I've found.

**½ stick cinnamon**
**6 whole cardamom pods**
**4 whole cloves**
**3 whole black peppercorns**
**450ml (16 fl oz) water**
**225ml (8 fl oz) milk**
**sugar, to taste**
**3 tsp black tea**

1. Lightly bruise the spices in a bowl with a large metal spoon.
2. Heat the water in a small saucepan, adding the spices and bringing to a gentle simmer for 8 minutes.
3. Add the milk and sugar to taste, stir and bring to a simmer again briefly.
4. Add the black tea, stir, turn the heat off and let it all steep for a couple of minutes.
5. Strain, and serve with a cinnamon stick for stirring.

# STORE-CUPBOARD INFUSIONS

Take a simple bottle of spirit and transform it into a deeply aromatic liquid with a rich, golden hue, or even inky black, and with myriad thrilling flavours. This elixir has versatile uses – it can be knocked back in a shot glass, or mixed up in cocktails, or gift-wrapped beautifully and given as a present. All this by simply raiding the kitchen cupboard and fridge for a few everyday ingredients.

Buy decent-quality base spirits for infusions at all times. This needn't mean premium vodkas or gin, by any means, but source relatively inexpensive versions only from a reliable shop with a high turnover, avoiding older bottles and the bargain basement (and the rough flavours that may ensue!). Vodka is the perfect base for many infusions as it tastes and smells almost neutral, letting the added ingredients shine through. Be aware that whisky, gin and brandy will impart more of their own characters to the finished drink, for better or worse.

The following recipes are based on ingredients that most of us have somewhere in the kitchen. Note: I've specified a standard 70cl bottle of spirit for each of these recipes, but you might have a little leftover each time. The important thing is to fill up your bottles or jars. Save the rest for cook's nips!

# Black Pepper Vodka

*Best enjoyed within 3 months*

Wow, this turns black as night within days and makes a really hot, spicy spirit. Don't attempt to sip it on its own, even cautiously – you might reel back, sneezing. But this is useful stuff for splashing into a Bloody Mary, or for pepping up a boring, healthy tomato or vegetable juice (see the tip on page 143 for making a Bloody Mary). Note: there's no sugar in this recipe – the aim is a very dry, intensely peppery liquid.

**100g (3½oz) black peppercorns**
**70cl vodka (unflavoured)**

1. Rifle through the peppercorns, removing any broken pieces and dust. You want whole corns.
2. Put the peppercorns into a large sterilized kilner jar and fill up with vodka.
3. Seal and shake gently to mix, then turn every day for 6 weeks to muddle up the peppercorns.
4. Strain off the peppercorns and discard. Bottle the black liquid.

* *For Bloody Mary mix: use instead of other hot, spicy ingredients, not with them! Make up the rest of the Mary, then add a dash of Black Pepper Vodka, taste and add a little more until you're happy with the balance.*
* *Chill in the refrigerator for a cooler mix with tomato/vegetable-based drinks.*
* *Use sparingly in rich gravies for roast beef, where it acts like a dab of horseradish; and you might put a shot into a spicy tomato chutney or piccalilli.*

# Coffee Bean Vodka

*Best enjoyed within 3 months*

Coffee liqueurs are hugely popular and have a warming quality. Here's a delicious, easy, home-made version, which is not cloying, creamy or over-sweet. Instead, it tastes of rich mocha with intense chocolate and burnt-toffee qualities, but with a sense of freshly roasted beans, too.

**60 coffee beans (I use good-quality, medium-strength Colombian)**
**1 heaped tsp sugar**
**70cl vodka (unflavoured)**

1. Tip the coffee beans into a large bowl and, using the back of a metal spoon, bash them until each one has cracked and broken a little.
2. Pour the cracked beans into a large sterilized kilner jar and sprinkle on the sugar. Top up with the vodka until full.
3. Seal and shake gently. Store in a cool, dark place, turning daily for 4 days. Strain and bottle.

* *Add to hot, strong black coffee and pour whipped cream on top, sprinkling with a little cinnamon.*
* *Clearly, this is a temptation with plain chocolate, ginger chocolate, chocolate coffee beans, chocolate-coated nuts, chilli chocolate. I could go on …*
* *Splash a little into rich meat stews (especially beef) for a Mexican hint of mocha that's barely discernible but nonetheless adds depth and power.*

# Star Anise Vodka

Great for creating a quick, perfumed, pastis-style spirit, to use up any pretty star anise leftover while Chinese cooking. The aniseed flavour is strong and natural, and very slightly sweet and spicy.

**25 star anise**
**70cl vodka (unflavoured)**

1. Place the star anise in a large kilner jar and pour on the vodka.
2. Seal, shake gently and leave for 3 days, turning twice a day.
3. Strain, bottle and enjoy within 4 weeks.

* *This tastes slightly medicinal (but in a good way), and seems to soothe a sore throat.*
* *Chill this and add cold water to taste and some ice cubes for an instant French pastis/Greek ouzo experience.*
* *Save the discarded star anise for cooking – chuck some in with roasting pork chops, or use in a Chinese-style marinade.*

# Vanilla Rum

*Enjoy within 6 weeks of bottling.*

An autumnal golden colour and slightly thickened texture mark out this tempting spirit infusion. Best enjoyed within a few weeks of making, as the truly lovely vanilla aroma does fade away with time. Note no sugar again – this does not need sweetening.

**4 vanilla pods**
**70cl white rum**

1. Slice open the vanilla pods with the point of a small, sharp knife and scrape out all the tiny seeds. Retain everything and chop the pods into 2cm (³⁄₄in) pieces.
2. Pour the rum into a large sterilized kilner jar and add the chopped vanilla pods and the seeds.
3. Stir with a long spoon to loosen the sticky seeds, then seal and turn gently to start the steep.
4. Leave in a cool, dark place for 6 weeks, shaking the jar gently from time to time.
5. Strain through very fine muslin and bottle in attractive containers.

* *This is an appealing shot on its own, slightly cool, preferably with a box of fine milk and white chocolates.*
* *Serve with creamy cardamom panna cotta, Turkish delight, or ginger desserts.*

# Spiced Rum

*Drink within 6 weeks of bottling.*

There are so many commercial spiced rums on the shelves these days, but it's surprisingly straightforward and quick to make your own. Do use golden rum instead of white though as the richer, more mellow flavour of the golden version counts for a lot here.

**70cl golden rum**
**1 vanilla pod**
**2 cinnamon sticks, broken in half**
**1 whole star anise**

**2 cloves**
**1 all-spice berry**
   **or 1 tbsp ground all-spice**
**2 large strips of rind from an orange**

1. Pour the rum into a large sterilized jar and add all the remaining ingredients.
2. Seal, shake gently and leave for 48 hours to infuse.
3. The spiced rum is then ready and you can strain off the solids at this point using a fine muslin to remove as much of the ground all-spice powder as possible. Or leave the spices in the rum for up to a week, but do strain it off at that point and bottle (see page 34).

* *A sweeter version can be made by adding sugar to taste at the initial infusion stage. I prefer this drier, however.*
* *Use in place of golden rum in cocktails and long drinks – it works well with ginger ale or tonic water, or to make Long Island Spiced Teas!*

# Cinnamon Schnapps

*Enjoy within*
*3 months*

You can use a clear, unflavoured schnapps or unflavoured vodka for this recipe, and even white rum works well. However, I think of this as less Caribbean and more Scandinavian. It's one of those shots that works well ice-cold on a freezing day. Standing in the snow, after singing Christmas carols, perhaps …

**3 cinnamon sticks**
**70cl unflavoured spirit**

1. Break up the cinnamon sticks roughly, and pop them into a large sterilized jar.
2. Pour on the spirit and shake gently.
3. Steep for a week, turning the jar daily.
4. Strain off the cinnamon and bottle (see page 34).

✳ *Use the larger pieces of cinnamon in a mulled red wine discarding any irritating tiny bits.*

✳ *Bottle in clear glass, tie a cinnamon stick with raffia to the neck and give away as a gift.*

✳ *Mix with ginger beer for a spicy, peppery kick.*

✳ *Make into a hot toddy by dashing Cinnamon Schnapps into a china cup, then adding a slice of lemon, 1 clove and a little honey. Top up with very hot water, stir and inhale the steam before you sip.*

# Cherry Brandy

*Drink within*
*6 months*

Christmas is the obvious time to drink (or cook with) cherry brandy, and beautifully wrapped bottles of a homemade version make particularly welcome presents. You could always give the brandy away while the cherries are still steeping in it, as they look so good, but do issue gentle instructions on when to remove the fruit.

**350g (12oz) fresh, ripe red cherries**          **1 tbsp caster sugar**
**1 cinnamon stick**          **70cl French brandy**

1. Wash the cherries and dry carefully. Remove any stalks and bruised fruit.
   Prick each cherry to help the juices start to flow.
2. Pack them into a sterilized kilner jar and pop the cinnamon stick on top.
3. Sprinkle the sugar over the fruit and top up to the brim with the brandy.
4. Seal and shake gently. Leave to steep for 6–8 weeks, turning the jar occasionally to mix.
5. Strain the fruit off after that time and bottle the brandy.

✳ *Savour on its own (at room temperature), with chocolate roulades and mousses, or Christmas cake.*

✳ *Use the brandy-soused cherries (after stoning) in fruitcakes, or chop up finely to add to mincemeat recipes.*

✳ *Or add more sugar to the stoned cherries and reduce a little Cherry Brandy to make a sauce for pancakes.*

✳ *Splash into gravy to enjoy with steak; homemade gravy with cherry brandy is also good with pork.*

# Cucumber Gin

*Drink within 6 weeks*

A big hit in our house. It's amazing how well the cucumber shines through the relatively strong flavour and aroma of gin. Cucumber gin is so scented, summery and refreshing and it makes a great cocktail ingredient. Use very fresh, crisp cucumbers, and always, but always, remove every scrap of the green peel, or the result might be bitter.

**3 small cucumbers**
**70cl gin (see below)**

1. Peel the cucumbers and slice them lengthways; take out the inner seed section of each one. Cut into 2cm (¾in) square pieces.
2. Put the cucumber pieces in a kilner jar, add the gin, seal, and shake gently to mix.
3. Steep for a week in a very cool, dark place, turning occasionally, then strain off the cucumber and bottle the gin.

✳ *Don't feel you have to use a premium gin for this, but do try to get one with more than 40% alcohol, as it will be an above-average spirit and one with more character. If you do want to use the very best, try Plymouth Gin or the already-rather-cucumbery Hendricks.*

✳ *You can drink this neat and very cold, especially in hot weather, but it is far better made into long drinks:*

   * *Try one part Cucumber Gin to two parts tonic water, with a sprig of bruised mint and plenty of ice.*

   * *Even better, one part Cucumber Gin, one part concentrated homemade Elderflower Cordial (see page 43) and two parts tonic, with mint and ice – a divine, cooling concoction, especially in high summer.*

   * *For a sweeter version of these cocktails, use lemonade instead of tonic water.*

   * *Cucumber Gin is also great topped up with dry ginger ale. Chill both ingredients.*

# FESTIVE DRINKS FOR ENTERTAINING

A truly festive drink is one for enjoying at precious moments when you're in a crowd, whether you are celebrating a ceremony such as Christmas, or treating a group of dinner guests at the end of a big feast, or kicking off a party in style. Boring, shop-bought, big-brand wines just don't cut it on a special occasion – so make something instead to show how much the moment means.

It was quite difficult to choose which drinks to put in this chapter, as we all have a different moment we consider to be the most festive, so I've included something for everyone (I hope!): a clever spiced syrup concentrate for that ever-popular winter warmer, Mulled Wine; Egg Nog for the same season but to satisfy those who adore passing round a creamy, rich liqueur; homemade Amaretto for those wonderful (and otherwise expensive) after-dinner digestifs; and a new take on a key ingredient for original Bloody Mary. Oh, and a soft, fizzy, but surprisingly healthy homemade 'soda' for kids' celebrations. Let's party!

# Mulled Wine and Mulling Syrup

*Makes 450ml*
*(¾ pint)*

*Keeps for*
*2–3 months*
*in a dark*
*store cupboard*

Hot, spicy, aromatic mulled wine is a true festive treat. But watch out: commercial mulled red wines or kits for making them often turn out horribly sweet or overladen with oily clove. Teabag-style sachets don't quite cut it either, with one or two honourable exceptions. Anyway, it's more fun to make your own concentrated base for hot, spicy mulled drinks. This recipe is adapted from one by Lulu Grimes – it makes the house smell wonderfully Christmassy while it's being concocted.

Simply reheat the quantity of mulling syrup shown below with a 75cl bottle of decent red wine or cider, adding a few fresh citrus slices to the pot. And don't forget to boast loudly that you made it all yourself.

**250g (9oz) caster sugar**
**2 ripe, juicy oranges, cut into quarters**
**6 whole cloves**
**6 allspice berries or 1 tbsp ground allspice**
**2 cinnamon sticks, broken in half**
**2 tsp freshly ground nutmeg**
**5cm (2in) fresh ginger root, peeled and sliced**
**1 litre (1¾ pints) cold water**

1. Put all the ingredients into a large pan and bring to just below the boil, stirring well to dissolve the sugar.
2. Simmer gently to reduce by half. Stir from time to time.
3. Leave to cool and then strain through very fine muslin twice before bottling.

* *Don't worry about the finished syrup being slightly cloudy – this is normal and won't show up once your red wine or cider and fruit are added.*

* *Use medium-bodied, ripe and hugely fruity red wine for mulling (and a fresh bottle: no dregs, pur-leeese).*

* *Add a good slug of brandy or port for an extra kick, if you like.*

* *When you come to make the final mull, never let it boil, as the alcohol will dissipate and it might taste slightly burnt and jammy.*

* *Serve the finished mull in thick glass tumblers, and give guests a cinnamon stick to stir their drink with.*

* *Try a White Wine Mull using a fairly rich, juicy white, such as Chardonnay, Viognier or South African Chenin Blanc as the base. Add a couple of star anise and two-thirds the quantity of mulling syrup (above) to 75cl white wine and honey to taste. Heat very gently.*

* *A 'Mock Mull' is a great soft version. Heat up homemade Blackberry or Blackcurrant Cordial (see page 66), diluted to taste, or red grape juice (see page 106), or buy some in if you are really stuck), and add star anise, cinnamon, honey and cloves, tasting as you add the spices bit by bit until you get the right balance. This goes for any mull – if in doubt, introduce the other ingredients to the liquid slowly, and taste regularly until the right flavour is achieved.*

* *Also try other mulled recipes: Cider on page 94 and Mead on page 112.*

# Egg Nog

*NB: this recipe contains raw egg*

*Makes approx 1 litre (1¾ pints)*

*Keep in the refrigerator until the 'best by' date on the fresh ingredients*

Given the current craze for keeping chickens, there are a few people with a ludicrous oversupply of eggs who can't give them away to their equally eggs-cessive neighbours. Don't make yet another omelette – try a homemade Egg Nog. Beware: this is very sweet (all that sugar!), strong (rum and brandy!) and rich (oceans of cream!). It's decadent, but oh-so good. This makes enough for a small crowd.

**6 fresh, free-range eggs**
**200g (7oz) caster sugar**
**1 tsp freshly grated nutmeg, plus more to garnish**
**½ tsp vanilla extract**
**500ml (18fl oz) double cream**
**400ml (14fl oz) full-fat milk**
**110ml (3¾fl oz) dark rum**
**110ml (3¾fl oz) brandy**

1. Beat the eggs well in a large bowl until frothy, add the sugar and beat again, then add the nutmeg and vanilla and mix well.
2. Now beat in the cream, followed by the milk and finally, trickle in the rum and brandy, bit by bit, mixing all the time.
3. Store in the fridge for a couple of hours to chill. Pour into glasses and grate a little nutmeg on top to garnish before handing round.

* *Make sure to pour the cream and milk, and then the rum and brandy, slowly and gradually to avoid the possibility of curdling.*
* *Serve in small amounts as this is so rich – a little glassful per guest does just fine.*

# Cumin Lassi

*Makes 650ml (just over 1 pint)*

*Always keep Lassi in the refrigerator and use within 2 hours of making*

Now for a healthy, cooling drink or two that works brilliantly when you've got friends or family visiting and want an alcohol-free but impressive option. Yoghurt-based, cooling Lassi is a traditional drink of the Punjab, and one that manages to create something moreish and deeply refreshing out of the most unpromising ingredients. Lassi can be alluring, especially in hot, humid weather, or to go with a light, healthy lunch. I've been through diverse recipes, including versions made with thick, rich yoghurt and even cream, but this Cumin Lassi and the variations that follow it (two salty and one sweet) are my favourites: I make no claims for the authenticity of these recipes, but they do taste good!

**1 heaped tsp cumin seeds**
**300ml (½ pint) plain, low-fat yoghurt**
**300ml (½ pint) semi-skimmed milk**
**2 tsp lemon juice**
**large pinch of fine salt**
**1 small teacup of ice cubes**
**fresh mint sprigs (optional garnish)**

1. Roast the cumin seeds in a dry frying pan for a few minutes, until they are just turning brown and giving off a rich aroma.
2. Pour them into a mortar and crush them up with a pestle.
3. Put in a blender with all the other ingredients, including the ice cubes, and whizz.
4. Pour into tall cold tumblers. You might like to garnish the lassi with fresh mint.

* *This works well when entertaining as it's quick and easy to whip up. I find 'ladies who lunch' love Lassi!*
* *To make a Saffron Lassi, use the recipe above, but with half the cumin. Soak 15 strands of saffron in 750ml warm milk and leave to soak for 1–2 hours. Add this to the blender with the other ingredients.*
* *For Mint Lassi, use the recipe above, but substitute 2 tbsp fresh, finely chopped mint leaves for the cumin.*

# Mango Lassi

*Makes 550ml (1 pint)*

*Always keep lassi in the refrigerator and use within 2 hours of making*

A delicious, refreshing treat. Young and old love it, so make it when your family piles round.

**300ml (½ pint) plain, low-fat yoghurt**
**200ml (7fl oz) fresh, ripe mango pieces**
**1 small teacup of crushed ice**
**2 tbsp caster sugar**

1. Chop the mango pieces very finely, retaining the juice that comes out.
2. Place all the ingredients in a blender and whizz until smooth.
3. Pour into chilled tall glass tumblers.

* *Make sure the mango you use is properly ripe; buy in advance and ripen at home, then leave out in a warm room before cutting it up. Underripe fruit will ruin the drink.*

# Amaretto

Not only is the almond-rich, fragrant amaretto liqueur a popular digestif, but it is also a versatile cooking ingredient and great in cocktails too. So, here's a dead-easy recipe for homemade amaretto. The real thing is created with oil of apricot kernels or almonds, or both; a natural almond essence is used here instead – make sure this (and the vanilla extract) are top-quality – no fakes! I have to say how impressive this drink is for the minimal effort required.

*Makes 650ml*
*(just over 1 pint)*

*Keeps well for*
*3 months*

**220ml (7½fl oz) water**
**200g (7oz) sugar**
**100g (3½oz) demerara sugar**
**37.5cl vodka (unflavoured)**
**50ml (2fl oz) natural almond essence**
**2 tsp natural vanilla extract**

1. Bring the water to the boil in a saucepan and add both the sugars. Take off the heat and stir well until the sugar is all dissolved. Leave to cool.
2. Add the vodka and stir. Add the two extracts and stir well.
3. Pour the amaretto into a jug, then through a funnel into a bottle and seal. The mix is ready to use right away.

* *The extracts will eventually separate whatever you do, so always shake or mix well, before using.*
* *Try a splash in creamy chocolate puddings, or poach peaches in a syrup containing a tablespoonful or two.*
* *Clearly, a sip of this is divine at the end of dinner, served with little crunchy amaretti biscuits.*

# Cherryade

*Makes 700ml*
*(just over 1 pint),*
*before diluting*

*Best enjoyed as*
*soon as it is made*

A versatile one, this – on its own, it's a tangy, pink drink for adults and kids, and best served outdoors in the garden or on a picnic. But you can also dash in spirit to make it into a delectable, alcoholic summer cocktail. Cherries have a unique, fragrant appeal, and this drink is lightly perfumed and deeply refreshing. Do I really need to say that it's way better than the fiercely fizzy, artificially flavoured sodas?

**225g (8oz) fresh, ripe cherries**
**600ml (1 pint) boiling water**
**1 lime**
**50g (1¾oz) caster sugar**
**sparkling water, to dilute**

1. Wash the cherries carefully and remove all stalks. Chop each one in half and remove the stones. Put the fruit in a big bowl and bruise them slightly with the back of a metal spoon to get the juices flowing.
2. Pour the hot water over the cherries and stir.
3. Peel the lime, and quarter it. Add a couple of strips of peel and the juice of one quarter to the cherries.
4. Add the sugar and stir until it is dissolved. Cover and leave for 2 hours.
5. Strain. Add cold sparkling water to dilute to your own taste.

* *There's an old tradition for using a tarragon sprig in this recipe – it adds a light aniseed note. If you want to do this, squash the tarragon leaves gently and add at stage 3.*
* *If you're heading away from home for a picnic, pack the cherry base and the cold sparkling water separately and make up the drink when you're settled down.*
* *For a long Cherry Cocktail, add a splash of good Cognac to each glass of the cherry base before topping-up with just a little sparkling water. Garnish with a twist of lime peel.*
* *You can use an orange or mandarin instead of lime here, but the sharp bite of lemon tastes wrong.*
* *This works pretty well with cherries that have been tinned in fruit juice, too – use the pitted cherries from a 425g tin, and approximately 4 tablespoons of the juice inside. However, fresh cherries are loads better.*

# Red Chilli Sherry

*Store in the refrigerator, for up to 4 weeks*

This was recommended to me by Angus McCaig, who runs The Holt gastro-pub in Honiton, Devon. The Holt specializes in smoked food of every variety, and Angus uses smoked chilli peppers for his sherry infusion – a fabulous drink with depth and intensity. However, fresh chillies are also great used in this infusion, and the result is the perfect ingredient for a Bloody Mary. I make it in small quantities because it doesn't last well, and only a little is needed at a time. A good thing fino sherry often comes in half-bottles, then.

**1 smallish, medium-hot red chilli pepper, approximately 6cm (2½in) long**
**37.5cl pale, dry sherry (fino or manzanilla)**

1. Wash and dry the chilli pepper; cut off the stalk.
2. Slice into the sides a couple of times (do not remove seeds).
3. Pour out a little of the sherry into a clean jug to make room for the chilli.
4. Push the chilli down the neck of the bottle and into the sherry.
   If it won't fit, cut it lengthways.
5. Top up with the sherry from the jug and reseal with the original cork stopper.
6. Shake gently, and leave to steep for 2–3 weeks, turning occasionally or whenever the mood takes you.
7. Pour some sherry out retaining it, remove the chilli using a metal kebab stick and discard. Top up and seal.

* *Cheaper dry sherry, as long as it's freshly opened and youthful, is fine for this; there's no point in splashing out on a fine label.*

* *The chilli looks fabulous while in the bottle – display the steeping infusion!*

* *This also adds a great kick to gazpacho or cold tomato soup. Go steady, though, as it's strong.*

* *Red Chilli Sherry isn't too nice on its own, unless you crave a very spicy shot. But added to a Bloody Mary or other tomato/vegetable juice base, it's just great. Add dash by dash, as you would with bitters to a cocktail mix, tasting until it's just right. It's important (nay, crucial) in life to know how to make a superlative Bloody Mary. Here goes:*

  *Fill tall tumblers with ice.*
  *Pour a large shot of good unflavoured vodka into each one.*
  *Mix up a jug of mainly tomato juice, with a good twist of white pepper, a large pinch of celery salt, the juice of half a lime and a splash of your homemade Red Chilli Sherry (see above).*
  *Stir, taste, adjust seasoning and add more lime juice and/or fino if needed.*
  *If you like a socking great spicy kick, dash in a few drops of Tabasco. Stir again.*
  *Pour this mix into the tumblers, over the vodka.*
  *Hand around with small sticks of celery as stirrers.*

  *I've tried making my own tomato juice, but the shop-bought stuff is excellent and cheap anyway. Concentrate on making the Red Chilli Sherry instead.*

# ENJOYING YOUR DRINKS

## SERVING

No one with any sense would uncork Champagne that was warm, or offer a ripe red Burgundy from a shot glass. Homemade drinks need serving the right way too, which is not to say you need to make a great fuss about them, but following a few simple 'rules of thumb' will help you get the best out of each one.

## STAY COOL

Almost all the drinks in this book taste much better when they are served properly chilled. Chilling a drink emphasizes its refreshing, mouthwatering acidity. This goes for the fermented Fruit Wines, Citrus Cordials, Orchard Drinks, Grape Drinks, Lassis and Floral Drinks except Rose Teas. The Infusions are a matter of personal taste - I prefer my Cucumber Gin very cold, but Damson Gin at room temperature, for example. To make a long drink taste even colder, chill the mixers and even the glasses.

## CLOSING-UP TIME

Don't open any homemade drinks before you need to - there are no heavy, tannic wines in this book, or indeed anything that benefits from 'breathing'. Homemade drinks tend to be more delicate than shop-bought wines, so minimize oxidation (the deteriorative effects of oxygen on wine). Only open and serve your drinks at the last possible minute.

## DRINKING-UP TIME

If you're serving drinks that have been opened on previous occasions, check them for freshness. Homemade wines, ciders and juices can be rather fragile and, without artificial preservatives or sulphur, they clearly don't keep well after opening. All in all, don't expect opened bottles to taste great three weeks after your last party!

## READY, STEADY, POUR

Have all your accessories ready in advance of pouring - that means not only cleaned and polished glasses but trays, stirrers, fruit and knives for chopping and other garnishes. More on these items follows, but the most basic rule of serving well is to be prepared.

# Glasses

It's the same for almost all fine drinks, homemade or otherwise – the best glasses for the job are, er, glass (not plastic or laminated paper); thin, as this feels nicer on the lips than thick glass; long stemmed, so you can hold the glass without warming up the liquid, and easily see the glints of colour and light in it; and plain, because cut crystal or coloured glass obscures your view of the drink's appearance.

So, simple, good-quality, tall wine glasses are perfect for all the homemade wines and cordials in this book, and they also appeal for serving grown-up soft drinks, ciders and perries, too.

You might prefer proper pint or half-pint glasses for Nettle Beer, Orchard Drinks such as Cider, and even Mead – if so, clear, plain glass is still the way to go. Thicker, chunkier glass tumblers are needed for hot drinks, though, and these also look good for spirit infusions served 'on the rocks'. Use tall highball tumblers (ideally plain glass again) for long drinks, and don't shy away from proper Champagne flutes for sparklers such as elderflower bubbly or those diluted with fizzy water or soda. Tall, slim flutes are better than wide, flatter coupes, so bubbles don't disappear in a blink.

Okay, okay, for small children, or by the pool, or on a picnic, I find that clear plastic glasses are by far the best option – in general, far better than cardboard cups – for those moments when glass really isn't suitable.

Chill the glasses themselves for very cold drinks – the frosty effect looks great. Simply place them in the fridge for a good hour before using.

And a final word on washing up: don't use too much detergent! Soapy residue on glasses can ruin the flavour and scent of a delicate homemade drink, and it will kill any bubbles dead. Very clean glasses are important, of course, but a tiny amount of washing-up liquid and lots of hot water can go a long way. Always use clean linen tea towels for drying, and check that all traces of lipstick are gone at this stage.

# Accessories

Maraschino cherries, paper umbrellas, silver sparklers … put them right out of your mind (unless planning a 1980s revival night). Chic accessories for modern homemade drinks are low-key, subtle, simple and preferably all-natural. You might need all the help you can get convincing sceptics about the joys of Elderflower Cordial, Mead, or Oak Leaf Wine, so try some of the ideas opposite to liven up your concoctions.

# Tastings

If organising a proper tasting of homemade drinks, you'll need spittoons for those who don't want to swallow all the samples. Clean jugs or even glass vases or little buckets will do fine if you don't own proper spittoons, and you might want to put kitchen paper into the bottom of each container. If it's a serious tasting or competition, stock up on notebooks and pens.

# Gatherings

Find time to enjoy your homemade results in relaxed settings. When there's a crowd coming round, encourage everyone to help themselves. Set up a 'bar', with glasses, chilled mixers, fruit garnishes, mint – everything anyone could need. Show off your finest concoctions, then tell your guests to get on with it so you can have a good time, too. Do keep all drinks cool, perhaps by setting some bottles outside in cold weather, or filling large buckets with ice and pushing bottles in.

# Celebrations

Move back into centre stage for any toasts or special announcements – this is the time to crack open fresh bottles, sparkling or otherwise, even bringing out a clean set of glasses on a tray. Try (just ahead of the big moment) mixing your homemade drinks for this: a dash of Damson or Sloe Gin in Champagne flutes topped up with dry cava, for example, or elderflower spritzers for non-drinkers.

## ICE CUBES
Make them more interesting by using concentrated cordial or freeze water with tiny, perfect berries inside (redcurrants, baby gooseberries or raspberries, for example).

## FLOAT
Sprigs of little flowers such as elderflower or individual rose petals on drinks, as well as mint sprigs, all make attractive garnishes.

## GARNISHES
Fresh slices of citrus or apple are the easiest. Also try twists of peel pared away from unwaxed, organic limes, lemons, tangerines or oranges. Little bunches of baby redcurrants, or tiny individual berries bobbing about in sparkling drinks look good, too. Or balance a kiwi slice on the side of a glass, or make a slash in the bottom of a strawberry and stick that on.

## SALT OR SUGAR RIM
Try this on your cocktail glasses or tumblers for extra pizzazz! Pour some coarse-grained salt or caster sugar into a saucer, rub a slice of lemon or lime around the outside rim of the glass and turn it upside down to dip firmly in the saucer. Salt works best with refreshing, tangy, dry drinks such as elderflower-based cocktails or Rhubarb Wine - use sugar with sweeter drinks such as Strawberry Wine.

## STIRRERS
Simple but neat and natural stirrers for homemade drinks include small, hard celery sticks for a bloody Mary, and cinnamon sticks for hot toddies. Use your imagination - or invest in some long-handled, attractive teaspoons, especially if you are planning to try 'muddling' (bruising) mint leaves or citrus wedges.

# SPRING AND SUMMER ENTERTAINING

It's vital to keep drinks tasting fresh and cool when it's hot outside and guests are thirsty. Chill everything drinks, mixers, glasses twice as hard as usual, and only pull each item out of the fridge at the last minute. Keep bottles in the shade, or in proper or improvised ice buckets.

## KEEPING IT LIGHT

The right drinks for summer parties and picnics are the lighter, more gently aromatic, elegant styles, preferably with a good crisp streak of acidity, which emphasizes the refreshing quality in your wine, cordial, or long drink.
Think dry and medium-dry, light white and pink homemade wines, ciders, perries and, of course, cordials, plus cold lavender and cucumber infusions for drinks with a whistle-clean, mouthwatering finish.

## SOFT DRINKS

Don't ever forget to provide these as well as alcoholic drinks for guests in warm weather. And for the drinkers, dilute strong alcoholic drinks with loads of chilled sparkling water, lemonade or soda to counteract the heat. No one wants dehydration and an instant headache in the middle of the day.
Iced Mint Tea or Masala Chai (see pages 118-121) are great ideas, too.'

## ON A PICNIC

Take homemade concentrates and mixers separately and mix together in situ. Put the resealed bottles in a stream or pool to keep them cool and always cover up any sweet and aromatic drinks once opened to keep the wasps and flies away!

## FOOD

Delectable summer party snacks to enjoy with the homemade drinks from this book should be elegant and light - avoid very sweet or rich, spicy dishes.
Try light, savoury canapes, cold prawns and smoked fish, delicate little savoury pastries and tarts, sushi and fresh fruit.

# AUTUMN AND WINTER ENTERTAINING

When it's cold outside, think hot toddies or soothing and spicy drinks such as those made from ginger or based on strong, wintry spirits such as whisky and rum creamy egg nog or sweet and spicy amaretto. Homemade drinks should be heavily perfumed, rich and heart-warming. The best homemade wines for colder weather months are elderberry, blackberry and plum.

## INDULGE

Stock up on baby marshmallows, ground cinnamon and cloves for sweet, creamy and hot winter drinks. Grate chocolate and nutmeg on your drinks and stir them with cinnamon sticks or chocolate flakes.

## MULLS AND HOT TODDIES

Never boil these drinks too much or the alcohol will steam off and disappear into the night...

## NON-ALCOHOLIC

Don't forget to provide good winter drinks for children and teetotallers, such as Fruity Ginger Ale, or Cherryade, or Blackberry Cordial, or Pink Grapefruit and Pomegranate Cordial. Anything that looks darker, richer, pinker suits the winter.

## FOOD

Great cold weather party snacks to tuck into with these homemade drinks include mildly spiced vegetable samosas, chilli prawns, olives with plenty of garlic, salted nuts, charcuterie and dried or preserved fruits. And, with any sweet and (or) creamy drinks, chocolate, of course!

# MATCHING DRINKS WITH FOOD

We're all quite used to matching 'normal' shop-bought table wines to food these days, but what about homemade drinks? Some of them work just as well at the dining table, and make terrific partners for certain dishes or types of cuisine. Here are some suggestions of where to start.

## MEAT

| | Page |
|---|---|
| Blackcurrant Cordial | 54 |
| Crème de Cassis | 62 |
| All blackberry drinks | 66–9 |
| Elderberry Wine | 70 |
| Red Grape Juice | 106 |

## CHICKEN, TURKEY AND DUCK

| | |
|---|---|
| Plum Wine | 58 |
| Oak Leaf Wine | 75 |
| All Orchard drinks | 90-101 |
| Parsnip Wine | 104 |

## FISH, SEAFOOD, VEGETABLE AND SALADS

| | |
|---|---|
| All elderflower drinks | 43–5 |
| Dandelion Wine | 46 |
| Gooseberry Wine | 57 |
| Plum Wine | 58 |
| Rhubarb Wine | 60 |
| All citrus cordials | 83–7 |
| Fruity Ginger Ale | 113 |
| Ginger Beer | 114 |

## SPICY FOOD

| | |
|---|---|
| Plum Wine | 58 |
| Mandarin and lime cordial | 84 |
| Lime, Ginger and Lemongrass cordial | 86 |
| Rice and Raisin Wine | 108 |
| Fruity Ginger Ale | 113 |
| Ginger Beer | 114 |
| Cumin Lassi | 137 |

## CHEESES

| | Page |
|---|---|
| All elderflower drinks (mild cheeses and goats' cheeses) | 43–5 |
| Dandelion Wine (mild cheeses and goats' cheeses) | 46 |
| Plum Wine | 58 |
| Elderberry Wine | 70 |
| Nettle Beer | 74 |
| Oak Leaf Wine (smoked cheese) | 75 |
| Damson Gin | 77 |
| All Orchard drinks | 90–101 |
| Mead | 112 |

## DESSERTS

| | |
|---|---|
| Lavender Lemonade | 50 |
| Strawberry Wine (drink with fresh fruit) | 56 |
| Crème de cCassis | 62 |
| Crème de Mure | 68 |
| Rosehip Syrup | 72 |
| Damson Gin | 77 |
| Quince Vodka | 78 |
| Limoncello | 88 |
| Amaretto | 138 |

# MATCHING DRINKS TO THE OCCASION

Of course, it's your choice, but here are my suggestions for drinks that work especially well on certain occasions.

# SOURCES OF FURTHER INFORMATION

## Websites

Here, in no order of preference, are some of the websites that may prove useful when looking for drinks-making ideas. Some give the low down on how to make, ferment, infuse, etc, while others (especially the newspaper and magazine-based websites) will lead you to interesting drinks recipes from well-known food writers and chefs.

www.bbcgoodfood.com

www.brew-magic.com

www.brewuk.co.uk

www.britishlarder.co.uk

www.celtnet.org.uk/recipes

www.channel4.com/food

www.cottagesmallholder.com

www.danish-schnapps-recipes.com

www.guardian.co.uk/lifeandstyle/food-and-drink

www.marga.org/food

www.organic-cheese.co.uk

www.rivercottage.net

www.studentrecipes.com

www.telegraph.co.uk/foodanddrink

## Books

Every wannabe winemaker should try to get hold of the classic *First Steps in Winemaking* by C.J.J. Berry (Special Interest Model Books, new ed 2002). This is a great beginner's guide that has converted two or three generations to the cause!

Other useful references:

Wilson, C. *Favourite Country Wines and Cordials* J. Salmon Ltd, 2001

Garey, T. *The Joy of Home Winemaking* Avon Books, 1996

Pooley, M. & Lomax, J. *Real Cider Making on a Small Scale* Special Interest Model Books, 1999

Beauviale, A. *Mes Boissons Maison* Christine Bonneton, 2007

Diffords, S. *Cocktails* Sauce Guides, 9th ed 2010

Atkins, S. *Cocktails & Perfect Party Drinks* Quadrille, 2005

I also raided a selection of very old drinks-making books dating from the 1960s–80s and would like to thank those friends, neighbours and relations who loaned some of these.

# INDEX

## ACKNOWLEDGMENTS

Huge thanks to the whole team at Mitchell Beazley for all their input and energy, and to Noel Murphy for his truly lovely photography. I also raise my glass to the many kind neighbours who helped me with advice and/or produce, but particular mention goes to smallholder extraordinaire Sam Robson, and my local assistant on this book Julie Cooney, aka the queen of strawberry wine! Thanks too to Nick Borst-Smith and to Ian Kendall of Homebrew in Exeter. Finally, a toast to my country-loving, produce-growing, wild-foraging parents Brian and Pat who, sometime around 1975, persuaded a sulky 10 year old to help make dandelion wine…